LIFE PURPOSE SECRETS

10 Ways to Find Meaning In Times of Uncertainty

STEVE P. LAROSILIERE

CONTENTS

Part III
TRANSITIONING TO YOUR LIFE PURPOSE

DISCLAIMER

This book is written for informational purposes only. Every effort has been made to make this book as complete and accurate as possible. However, there may be mistakes in typography or content. Also, this book provides information only up to the publishing date. Therefore, this book should be used as a guide - not as the ultimate source.

The purpose of this book is to educate. The author and the publisher do not warrant that the information contained in this book is fully complete and shall not be responsible for any errors or omissions. The author and publisher shall have neither liability nor responsibility to any person or entity with respect to any loss or damage caused or alleged to be caused directly or indirectly by this book.

If you'd like to take advantage of more help in finding your life purpose, please visit our additional products and services at www.lifepurposesecrets.com

For Ashley, Toren, Zavier, and Amelie... this is for you.

INTRODUCTION

Your life purpose is beyond finding something to occupy your time. It's about reaching for goals that focus on growth and self-development. "It should be an opportunity for adventure and discovery," says Fred Silverstone, a licensed mental health counselor with Harvard-affiliated McLean Hospital. Have you ever wondered why you are in this world? Does it occur to you that we are all in this life to fulfill a purpose? To find it and solve the puzzles of life.

The sad truth is some of us live our entire lives trying to figure out the purpose of our existence. Some people fail, others succeed. Some find their purpose, yet get diverted from it. When you know your purpose in life, there is a higher chance of living a more meaningful life than others who don't. You are likely to live each day to the fullest because you know where you're going.

According to Eleanor Roosevelt, "The purpose of life is to live it, to taste experience to the utmost, to reach out eagerly and without fear for a newer and richer experience." Humans want to live life and taste all the experiences that come with it. Circumstances and situations stand in our way—stopping us in our tracks. Yes, some were faced with all of these yet succeeded. They were all open to the opportunities and experiences presented to them and achieved their life goals by working hard. They found purpose.

People who found purpose had a few things going for them —they had a support system, a path and system for replicating success, or they had the determination to succeed. They leveraged those assets to overcome the challenges and obstacles they encountered on their journey.

They did not find success by accident. They had it planned and executed it flawlessly. They were intentional about it. Mastered the art of due diligence before embarking on any causes, projects, ventures, or businesses. When you have access to mentors, resources, visualization, and alternate pathways when encountering roadblocks, success is inevitable. Scrolling through life is unacceptable. You need clear understanding of your ability to learn and grow. You also need to know your strengths, weaknesses, and goals.

Finding purpose is about understanding what makes you fulfilled. It starts with passion, but you have to unpack it— "unpack it" means being clear about what you are passionate about—then pursue it obsessively as if your life depended on it. Have you ever asked yourself if finding purpose was really important? Is it something that is just made for people in movies or books? If you're reading this, do things feel a little out of your control? Or does it feel shaky and uncertain as if you cannot even imagine what the next six months would look like?

Perhaps life didn't end up the way you had hoped. Does achieving your goals seem so far off that you don't even know how you'd go about them? Maybe you've dabbled into some self-work and personal development. Or you've had a bad experience, and you were very skeptical about it. I have been there, and trust me, it can be so confusing. But there is a set of tools and resources—which you will get in the book—that you can draw inspiration from if you are ready to change this narrative.

Once you've found your purpose, you'll notice how distinctly different and easy life is for you than others. Your purpose is yours alone, and it doesn't have to be for other people. Before we get started on the book, I want to share a bit of my story. I remember being in my late twenties, right after the attacks of 9/11. I lived in New York City, Brooklyn, to be specific.

I was running a marketing company with a business partner. I just witnessed and lived through one of the worst tragedies that had happened on US soil—many lives were lost, and a sad tale is not something I would love to tell. Our office was just a few miles away from ground zero. The highway led from the Brooklyn Bridge, coming from downtown, was called the Brooklyn / Queens Expressway—and it was shut down. The only vehicles that were allowed to go on the expressway were emergency vehicles coming from ground zero.

As my old business partner and I struggled to go back to work and maintain some sense of normalcy, we were reminded of how tragic the environment was. Every 20 to 30 minutes, an ambulance would go by with dead bodies being evacuated from ground zero—a constant reminder of the grim situation we were up against.

It took me several years to realize what had happened to me. I went through a lot of trauma—like many others. I couldn't articulate my state of mind; a lot was on my mind—including obsessively watching the news, going to dark negative places in my mind, smoking marijuana in excess, and drinking lots of alcohol as a coping mechanism. I was searching for answers, but I couldn't find any. I'd just witnessed a lot of people who lost their loved ones and jobs. Then my mind started playing tricks on me. I began to think the same was going to happen to me, anxiety and depression crept in. I found myself crying a lot, and I didn't understand why. I remember being just sad all the time. All I wanted was to lock myself up in the closet, throw a cover over and cry myself away.

I knew something had to change, but I didn't know what. One fateful day, on my way to my office, I saw a man selling books on the subway. He asked me if I wanted to buy his book. I said no. That didn't deter him as he went about his business, asking everybody in the subway car the same question. I overheard him telling someone that he'd written the book and that got me curious. The first thought that came to my head was, "what nerve does this guy have to write and sell his book on the subway?" So I decided to follow him.

We coincidentally got off at the same subway station. I felt compelled to walk up to him and ask about his book—since he had already piqued my interest, buying from him was a done deal. I found myself buying two books from him for $5. One of the books was about youth-serving nonprofits in the United States. The other book was called, "*No More Prisons*," written by Billy Upski Wimsatt and it talked about community activism, self-education, and mentoring.

After digesting the book's content, I realized it was speaking to me—as no other book had done–the part about mentoring sparked my interest. Wimsatt had 20 mentors at the time, and I was baffled at that number. I thought to myself, "What could I be if I had 20 mentors?" That was the question that changed my life trajectory and set me on a new path. I was eager to have a mentor—someone who has been successful that I could learn from.

Jeff Surut was the best fit, and I reached out to him. He owned a couple of bars in New York City, so I told him that I wanted him to be my mentor. He asked, "What's a mentor?" I replied, "I just want to have dinner once a month and talk about life."

The next thing I did was Google "Mentoring in New York

City." Then I came across a nonprofit organization ready to take me on, so I signed up. A week later, I began my training, and my first mentoring match was to mentor a 15-year-old kid in foster care. I figured that if I were benefiting from having a mentor, I would have a lot to offer to someone who was less fortunate. From that experience, I delved deeper, and became a mentor to many kids, motivating and inspiring them to be their best.

The second incident happened when I was into online networking and stumbled on the profile of life coach, Mieke Fruechtenicht. She was German but lived in New York City at the time. We met for coffee, and her amazing free spirit and energy were contagious. I wanted the same for my life. She eventually became my mentor and coach—even though I was completely oblivious to the event that led to it. When we sat down for my first mentoring session, she asked me a critical question: "What do you want in your life?" The way she asked this drew me in. It allowed me space to meditate and dig deeper into providing an answer that I had never articulated before. She gave me space mentally, physically and emotionally to be my true self.

The answer to that question led to a set of validation moments for finding my purpose. My answer was that I wanted to be in a community of highly motivated and creative individuals who wanted more out of life. I looked back to when I started my first business and how lonely it was, taking risks and doing things all on my own. I felt no support from any of my friends and family at the time. I knew that answer would set the course for who I wanted to be.

I wanted to do something that aligned with who I was, and somehow, I wanted to help people. I enjoyed the space and the freedom that she gave, which made me focus on reaching my goals. These two stories laid the groundwork for me to find my purpose. Since then, I've been able to impact the lives of thousands of people through mentoring. Currently, I'm on a new mission to help 10,000 people find their purpose. The same way that book inspired me to pursue my path, I hope this book will be the catalyst for you to pursue your dreams.

If you have been struggling to find your purpose in life with each passing day, I have good news. This book has the answers to all your life mysteries and the uncertainty that hangs over your head. Make a change today to turn your life around—it's all within your hands.

PART I
UNDERSTANDING LIFE PURPOSE

PREFACE

Why am I here? This is one of the most critical questions asked by anybody who has ever walked the earth. The question has baffled humanity from the beginning of time. After all, we didn't play any role in our existence. We didn't request to be born into this world. One day we appeared on this earth, and that was it. So, it is not out of place to ponder: Why am I here?

The truth is, humanity instinctively knows that the answer to this question is essential. We even have the answer at our finger-tips. Whether we believe it or not, our current path has been chosen based on the answer you have. The twist here is that a lot of people don't have an answer to it. It's not just high school or college graduates who have no answer to the critical question, "Why am I here?" You'll be surprised that many adults do not know why they are here on earth, even after having successful lives with businesses running on autopilot. There's still space for them to figure out the answer.

A lot of the conflict starts when adults "make it" or when there's a lot of chaos and uncertainty. The environment gives people room to think and ask questions like, "What do I want to do with my life? "What am I passionate about?" "What impact do I want to leave in the world?" "What are people going to say about me when I die?" "How can I make my life better?" Do these questions sound familiar? These are all questions that adults ask themselves to help clarify their purpose.

These questions come about when people still haven't figured out the answer to "why am I here?" Does it have to be this difficult to figure out? Well, it depends. We live in this world for an undetermined amount of time—which is not within our control. For some people, it is important how they spend their time, and for others, it is less important. What makes things more difficult is the lack of knowledge and self-awareness around what people should be doing with their time here on this planet. Some individuals base their lives and decisions on expectations, cultural norms and obligations. Eventually, this leads to a life of regret, and they never truly become themselves.

Meanwhile, people who set out to find themselves do it in a way that is not easy and often unpleasant. There are many obstacles along the way. When you pursue this path of finding your life purpose, your interests, passion, values, and beliefs must be your top priority. On this path, you will be looking out for things that truly make you fulfilled. That means you will lose people who do not add value to your life and add people who do.

Pursuing your purpose is oftentimes fearful and confusing and can lead to misunderstandings and self-doubt. You will have to rethink many of your life choices and revisit some of the relationship decisions you made along the way. It is much like a spring cleaning of sorts that happens in your mind with what happens in the physical space, including relationships and current obligations. In doing so, you are one step closer to figuring out your life purpose. Finding life purpose is one of the many reasons there has been a lot of research on the impact of personal development and our relationship to social behavior. With the influx of technology, social media has put a spotlight on the individual and impacts how we communicate with the world. People become gradually curious about who they are.

The awareness of self has been one of the driving forces for people wanting to discover life purpose. One of the best ways to understand the definition of purpose is to know how different it is from goals. Purpose answers the "why am I here?" question and provides personal meaning. It is the context that defines your life goals. It's the central hub or operating system in your life that helps dictate the goals, gives you the meaning of existence and helps provide a framework for your behavior. Purpose guides your personal resources and channels them into your decisions and your goals. Rather than dictating your behavior, purpose provides you with directions and isn't any different from your car's navigation system.

You don't have to follow your purpose, but there are so many benefits attached when you do. You can tell the difference between someone that is following their purpose and someone that is not. The former is a life force. It's almost as if you can see it in their eyes and their behavior. These types of people have an impact on their environment and are aggressive in pursuing their goals. To this end, we must organize our lives and become more persistent as it relates to our time and the environment, we live in.

More than anything, life purpose is more about living life in a conscious way. That is why Winston Churchill succinctly said, "It's not enough to have lived. We should be determined to live for something." Look at it from this perspective: you have a good job, and you are well paid. If you're not making a difference, and it doesn't align with your core values and beliefs, then it's just a job.

You'll wake up in 15-20 years and realize you have lived a life devoid of purpose. You could end up staying in a job, relationship or business for so many years, and then you realize that it is not what you wanted in the first place. When you know your life purpose, you live life consciously. All of your actions, goals, and behaviors will happen such that you love every moment of it, even the difficult parts. You understand that your problems will not suddenly go away—they are there for a reason, and you need to be determined to find a solution to them.

1

HOW DO YOU FIND YOUR PURPOSE?

I t's already within you! "Finding" your purpose is a misleading concept because it's not something you have to go out and "get," but rather something you need to find within and claim. You've already got it, even if you haven't consciously realized or chosen it yet. Of course, whether you believe it is already within you or not, you still need to "find" it in some sense. How do you do that? By looking in the most obvious places – your passions and interests. Your purpose will always be something that you feel passionate about, naturally good at, already love to do, and important to you.

Why would you be given a life purpose that doesn't match the essence of who you are? Would the universe expect a musical prodigy to spend his life crunching numbers in an accounting firm? Would the universe expect you to wait tables when your true passion is childhood education? How would these situations serve anyone? They wouldn't! Your life purpose will also utilize your greatest passions, talents and interests. No exceptions. Does that inspire a little sigh of relief for you? It should. You need to uncover the clues that lead to your life purpose. Namely, things you are good at, feel passionate about, love to do, and are important to you.

How do you know you have discovered your life purpose? The answer to this question is not far-fetched. It is as simple as when you feel so motivated and energetic from all your activities. The grind and the inertia to get started on tasks go away, and you're so focused on the thing you want to do. Let me take it from a personal point of view, so you can understand it better. I was running the marketing company, and we were very much struggling to keep it alive. Our biggest client had just cut our monthly retainer fee. The reality is, we had to take pay cuts to keep the business going.

As tough as that was, I knew there was more to life at the time. Prior to that time period, I had come across the work of Robert Kiyosaki's *Rich Dad Poor Dad,* which gave a new perspective on several things. I started saving money, so I no longer "stressed" about the decrease in my income. Then I started spending more time mentoring a kid and having my own mentor, which gave me enough perspective and context to help figure out what was missing in my life.

So even though life was very difficult on the outside--on the verge of closing my company, and the economy was in a recession—I was excited about checking in with my mentee every Thursday from 3:30 to 5 p.m. I'd leave my office and go have a mentoring session with my mentee in foster care. My mentorship periods were some of my best moments—either as a mentee or mentor. I felt at peace with myself, and my life challenges seem lighter than air. I was providing value and getting the same in return. I was providing meaning for the child's life.

For an hour and a half every week, I didn't think about myself and my challenges, and I poured everything into him by being fully present, listening, offering advice, laughing and learning from each other. On a micro-level, I knew I had found my purpose, and the thing that I became obsessed with was around forming relationships that matter. I knew that my life was going to change, but I didn't know how. All I did know was that I wanted to surround myself with these kinds of quality relationships.

2

HOW DO YOU MEASURE LIFE PURPOSE?

W hen it comes to measuring your life purpose, there are a few things to consider. The first is sacrifices. Any work you do as you're following your purpose involves making sacrifices. Everything comes at a cost, and not everything you do is going to be fun and easy all the time. So, the big question when pursuing your purpose is, what are you willing to sacrifice to get what you want? If you give up at the slightest hint of pressure or stress, then what you were pursuing is definitely not your life purpose.

However, if you are willing to stick through the rough times and go through it no matter what, then you may be in pursuit of purpose—or living on purpose. This shows that no matter what, your ability to be resilient, persistent, and even commit to something shows how much it means to you and how much you care. Let me give you a better explanation to drive home my point. Let's assume you are a salesman. Are you the type that will give up at the slightest rejection or go all the way after multiple rejections?

Marketing Donut, a small business marketing website, did a

breakdown of the average sales follow-up drop-off rate. That is, how many salespeople give up after each consecutive follow-up? Here's what they found: 44% stop following-up after one rejection. 22% stop following-up after two rejections. 14% stop following-up after three. 12% stop following-up after four. This means that an overwhelming majority (92%) of sales representatives give up before that crucial fifth follow-up. So that 8% of salespeople who do bother to follow-up five times are scoring more deals and making more bank than everyone else combined. In other words, 8% of reps are getting 80% of all sales.

You must be intentional about what you want— and criticism and rejection are part of the journey to finding purpose. Another example is when you aspire to be a writer, and you're afraid that people will criticize your work or express negative opinions about it, don't expect to go far with such a mindset. However, if you develop a winning mindset that allows you to keep going regardless of the challenges, you may well be on that path to fulfilling your purpose. Challenges will get in the way so you don't achieve your purpose—but you should see them as milestones and stepping stones to reaching your destination.

When I first started my organization, there was a paucity of funds, and I had to fundraise. I knew something had to happen if I wanted to move my organization forward. I got a spreadsheet and entered the names, addresses, and phone numbers of people who could help. Then I started making calls every day. I made my first call to a friend—using my elevator pitch— and she donated $50. So, I thought it was going to be an easy ride since the money came with less effort, but I was wrong. Then I proceeded to call everybody within my network, and was slammed with over 200 rejections. These people were my friends and family! Giving up was not an option.

I wanted to start a snowboard mentoring program for kids. The imagination was so strong that I saw a bus full of kids and mentors going snowboarding with a beam of smiles—with all the resources made available by me. My passion was snowboarding, and I wanted to spread the joy and love of the activity to black and brown kids so that they could enjoy the same lifestyle that I was so passionate about. I was fulfilling my purpose at that moment, and nothing was going to stop me.

Another way to measure purpose is if your job brings you so much joy and happiness that it feels like you are having fun with it. Like the popular quote, "Choose a job you love, and you will never have to work a day in your life." When you're living on purpose, you see life from a different perspective, so much so that you feel high and can't sleep at night. You even get so excited that people around you think that you're obsessed. The mere thought of what the future holds fills you with much happiness. You're constantly thinking about what's next and new ways to achieve great things.

As we grow and age, we lose sight of what was important to us. That childlike quality of being so curious and happy and joyful depreciates as we get beaten down by obligations, commitments, cultural norms, and our environment. A lot of social pressure causes us to lose passion and sight of who we are. In an effort for society to have "grownups," we lose who we are, and the school system is partly to blame. The American education system is not helping—it sucks out our creativity, and then we grow up with the belief that we're supposed to follow a predefined path, only to wake up much older, regretting a lot of our life decisions. Society tells us that there has to be a tangible reward for achieving anything meaningful: job title, salary, or status symbol. We go all out looking for physical rewards, forgetting what the experience is. By looking beyond, the "tangibles" and seeking the intangible--growing through skills, relationships, experiences, and going through that process--if you find your joy, then you may have found your purpose.

Coincidentally, one method that can point you in the direction of your passion is vulnerability. Vulnerability is a complicated thing. In a sense, it is easy to feel weak and get discouraged, but vulnerability often leads people to their sense of purpose. Purpose and passion are directly related and draw from connecting with and helping others overcome a battle that you have personal experience with. If you are passionate about something, remember that risk-taking is a necessary part of the journey. You need to take the risk to go out there and do what you love. Otherwise, you may need to revisit what your life purpose is if you're easily embarrassed as you make mistakes.

If you're living your purpose, you absolutely don't care what people think; you don't care what they say or get embarrassed. Even if you do feel those things, you do it regardless because you know that you will be miserable if you don't pursue this. You live with a mountain of regret, and you're willing to put yourself out there and take an enormous risk to achieve what you set out to do. You have to do what the 8 percent of goal-setters—the successful ones—do consistently and exceptionally well. Research by Edwin Locke and Gary Latham found that when people followed two principles –setting specific and challenging goals -- it led to higher performance 90 percent of the time. You just need to be ruthless when it comes to taking risks to achieve your life purpose.

One thing that I did when I first started my organization was emailing all of my contacts to tell them that I was quitting my job and was going to start a snowboard mentoring nonprofit organization. The year prior to quitting, I built up a large network of like-minded individuals, and I broadcasted it to the world that I was going to do this. Only my close friends and family knew the major sacrifices that I was making, but to other people, I was just doing something rather unique and extraordinary. I was so scared; I didn't know what I was going to do. I didn't know how to do it. I barely knew how to start, but putting myself out there to my whole community made me vulnerable, and I felt compelled to follow through on my dream.

When people don't know what's important to them, it's hard to get a real sense of direction or purpose, and when you don't have any purpose and direction, you're subject to the whims, ideas and opinions of other people. The next thing you know, people's values and beliefs are put on to you, and you're living someone else's life instead of living your own. Many adults still take on the beliefs and values of family and tradition, even though it's not something that they absolutely 100% buy into.

When you grow in an uncertain and stressful environment— be it the state of the world or politics or the economy—and you're consuming the views in the media and other people without any checks and balances, you're heading towards a directionless existence. I could remember the response I got from people when I told them about starting my first organization. The negative words came in numbers. Even friends and family wanted me to get a job first, make some money, before starting up my nonprofit.

That didn't seem like a bad idea to me, but I have a mind of my own, and I felt I should start ignoring a lot of beliefs and opinions that didn't align with my goal. It should be more of what I want to be doing and not what they think I should be doing. I had to shut them off and take out those negative opinions about what I set out to do. My vision was so clear that sometimes it kept me awake all night. I was obsessed with the idea, and I knew that my life would be different if I could take a giant leap forward and put myself out there, doing something much bigger than me in order to serve others.

Now my challenge was I didn't know how, but I knew I needed to make a significant change for my life to have real meaning. I was tired of using other people's definitions of success. I didn't want to become successful and later regret that I'd made the wrong decision. I wanted to make "giving back" a part of my success and find fulfillment in doing so. This is why I wrote this book, so you can have the tools to help you find your life purpose and start taking control of your life and business to make the most significant impact on the world.

3

PURPOSE VS. GOALS

We hear the words "purpose" and "goals" frequently used in our daily lives, but do we know what they mean and how they are the same or different? Someone recently asked me if lacking a goal means the same thing as lacking a purpose. The answer is no — it is not the same at all. Purpose and goals are almost similar, and one could hardly come across any difference between the two at one glance. Purpose and goal are interlinked, which makes it hard to make out the difference between the two.

One of the main differences between the two is the time factor. People try to reach their goals by setting deadlines. On the other hand, deadlines do not apply to a purpose. Goals are specific and focus on actual behaviors. It is a particular endpoint and serves as a framework on the actions that take you away or towards its final endpoint. Purpose, on the other hand, is broader and is the catalyst for the behavior and fuels the creation of your goals. It isn't about guiding you towards a specific outcome, but more about motivation and inspiration to be more goal-oriented. Values and the purpose that come from it point you in the right direction and are very different from a goal's specificity.

Purpose is somewhat the manager of all goals. People who

have a sense of purpose can move from one goal to another and have the capacity to manage multiple goals simultaneously. Those without a purpose in life may be able to achieve a single goal, but right after that, they are stuck and struggle to identify what's next. Consequently, goals act as a target and are motivated by your purpose.

There are three dimensions of purpose—strength, scope, and awareness. Scope infers the impact of purpose on your life. Goals that prompt your emotions, thoughts, and behaviors are said to have a broadening scope. A narrowly focused purpose causes more organization, but it doesn't impact a wide range of behaviors compared to a full reached purpose. A full reached purpose will influence your thoughts, emotions and actions.

Strength allows your purpose to impact your emotions, thoughts, and actions within the context of its scope. A well-defined purpose has an impact on your behaviors. If you put that side-by-side with scope and strength, it will dictate how long your purpose impacts your well-being and longevity. A purpose with a large scope and enormous power can have a lasting impact on your life. A broad purpose allows you to become more resilient to overcome challenges and obstacles that pave your path to success. The more aware you are, the better you can articulate your purpose. Always remember that strength and scope will influence your purpose to a large extent.

Let's paint a perfect picture with the analogy of wireless technology. In the United States, wireless technology is everywhere—its scope is broad. As long as we go to areas where there's a Wi-Fi signal, and you have gadgets that can connect to the internet, we can search the internet as much as possible. It has been implanted in our subconscious that we can get online whenever and wherever we are. Imagine being in a third-world country or a rural community, where there is less wireless access. At that point, you are instantly reminded that it's not business as usual. Your subconscious is "reconfigured" into believing that things have changed. Then your self-awareness kicks in. Next time you want to connect to the internet, your reconfigured subconscious will alert you that you have to contend with the challenges that come with less wireless access. Your behaviors will then conform to embracing the challenges at hand.

Behaviors that are motivated by purpose can be "switched on" to take action. As you become acutely aware of your purpose, you'll need significantly less effort to start embarking than if you were unaware.

4

THE IMPORTANCE OF FINDING MEANING IN LIFE

Society says that when you achieve success, you'll be happy. We know better. That is the wrong ideology. The alternate approach would flip that perspective all over. Even when we have achieved happiness, we still feel we are missing something. What if there is something much deeper than happiness that brings us fulfillment? That's where finding meaning in life comes into the picture. Finding meaning is as important as that happiness you seek. Once you find meaning in life, then long-lasting and consistent happiness becomes yours. You'll also enjoy happy relationships and a job you love so much.

Have you heard about living a conscious life? Well, I will demystify it here. Many experts say that there are two ways to live life. The first way is awareness of consciousness, which means that you live in synchronicity with others. You'll experience the same things in a different manner. The second way to live is by living unconsciously. When you live in an unconscious way, life happens to you. I see it like a wind blowing you in different directions, yet you have no power to resist—you just obey and flow through. You have no mind of your own. The only thing you are conscious of is where the wind takes you. Nobody wants to live life this way, but sadly, that is the reality for many folks—it is such a bizarre way to live.

According to well-being researcher, Laura King, "…lives may be experienced as meaningful when they are felt to have significance beyond the trivial or momentary, to have purpose, or to have a coherence that transcends chaos." Living a meaningful life is never about the moment or trivial issues. Learning the meaning of life gives you more clarity as to what your purpose is. The more you learn and understand yourself, the more clarity you have about why you are in this world. You'll dread waking up in the morning if you don't know what your purpose is. Even the start of a new week will be torturous for you because you're only looking forward to the weekend. You'll get overwhelmed and stressed you attempt any challenging situations. If you live a meaningful life, the struggle becomes fun—you may even ask for it every day, as it builds your mental resilience.

"Her clarity gave her purpose, and her purpose gave her clarity."
-Jonathan Stroud

From the quote, clarity can lead you to your purpose and then give your life meaning. We tend to get carried away with all the noise and confusion in the world. That should not impede our progress. A lot of people tend to have shiny object syndrome. Some common themes include a new business opportunity, more money, a new house, new car, new diet, the newest phone and other material objects of great interest. Come to think of it: how many of those things are important in the long run? Have you thought of something you're passionate about? Have you thought of something that you love doing? Or something that lights you up?

It's interesting how people who become wealthy tend to seek more meaning and purpose in their own life after they've attained wealth. They seek spirituality; they do more phil-anthropic work and personal development to make a bigger and broader impact. Here is the thing—you can impact your world without being wealthy or rich. What matters is the desire to change lives and make it worth living. Finding your life purpose will help you become acutely aware of what is important and not important in life.

When you look past the unimportant material, you will see what is absolutely necessary to be happy and fulfilled. It will give you clarity on your goals and help eliminate everything that isn't adding value to your life or steals you away from your purpose. If you are seeking your purpose, you have to keep pressing towards the goal—don't give up. The way to go is having clear filters on what is important vs. unimportant. This action will save you several years of wasted effort and help you become happier in the long run.

When you eventually find what is important to you, you'll be able to cut through the noise and confusion that the world throws at you and find meaning for your life. When you move in that direction, you'll have new definitions of success. What is success to one person is not for the next person. Whether it is building schools in third world countries, helping people over-come trauma and loss, or creating the next piece of technology, success is unique and personal to every individual. Having meaning in your life is both unique and fulfilling. Each moment, each interaction, and each day is an opportunity to be the best version of yourself. Every moment should gravitate toward becoming a better person, which opens up doors to living the best life there is. You need to understand that success will only lay on your lap when you find meaning in life.

Let's look at the role of clarity. Being clear about your life sounds great, but there is more to it than helping you find purpose. Here are more reasons why gaining clarity is important:

- Clarity minimizes doubt and increases self-confidence.
- Frustration will cease when you are clear because you are less confused.
- It can help you to learn your strengths and work on your weaknesses while you go through the process of self-reflection to find clarity.
- Help you set real goals that will make you take action.
- You can make better (and faster) decisions, which match your core values.
- Clarity helps when you're usually stuck in a rut or when you feel stuck in life.
- Happiness and satisfaction are common occurrences in your life when you are clear.
- Clarity brings greater energy and focus to your day.

Has it crossed your mind that external factors and the environment could be defining your current situation? If you have had sleepless nights over this, then perhaps you're a long way off figuring out what your purpose is in life. When you lack meaning in your life, your environment starts to shape you. The people around you start to shape your ideas and set the level of your ambition and your daily beliefs. You'll find yourself in a bunch of unfulfilling jobs and relationships. Everybody wants fulfillment in life. Otherwise, you're probably stuck in a business that you hate or a job that makes you feel stuck—or even unhealthy relationships.

Before I found purpose, I didn't have a clear sense of where I was going. Working and making money was all I could think of, and I felt that was what my life was about. I was stuck in a rut—

the more I tried to get out, the more I got stuck. Even a 7-year relationship never brought fulfillment. My life centered on watching TV and drinking to unwind. During the weekends, I would go shopping to get some home essentials. There was nothing extraordinary to look forward to, and I felt there was more to life than what I had at the moment. At the age of 27, I had built a successful company and pretty much had all I wanted. Something was lacking, and I knew I had to change to fix this feeling.

When I started to gain clarity, and my purpose came to the forefront, all my decisions started to make sense, and the changes started to align with who I wanted to be. Even though it was pretty tough to make this change, I knew that was what I needed, and the help of mentors (some had gone through a similar experience) was vital at this stage. When you're living a meaningful life, the things that bring fulfillment can also become your passion, and that can lead to purpose. So, I started to pursue snowboarding a lot more. A few years earlier, I had bought a snowboard on a whim because a friend did it. It was always something that I wanted to do.

As I ended my engagement, I saw the snowboard in my living room one evening, noticing that it hadn't been used in a year or two. In a moment of desperation, I thought to myself, "If I could do anything right now, what would I do?" My thoughts ran wild, and boom, snowboarding came to mind, specifically, the thought of visiting my Uncle Eddy in British Columbia and going snowboarding at Whistler. It was on that trip that I came up with the idea for my nonprofit. I met up with my coach and mentor and revealed exactly how it felt to have this idea, and she simply said, "Do what feels good." Little did I know that snow-boarding was going to change my life.

So, if you are looking for meaning and purpose, look at the things that you enjoy, whether it is sports, working out, reading, business, or personal development. Dive right into those interests and be selfish about it. You'll be able to find more meaning and purpose, cutting out toxic and unhealthy people in the activities.

As soon as you take that bold step and pursue purpose, the desire fuels within you. It makes you a lot lighter, happier and more joyous when around people. People then gravitate towards you, ask your opinion on things, and seek your help and guidance. Living a more meaningful life is not all about rainbows and unicorns. It can be stressful and demanding. It also requires a lot of energy and commitment. You must learn to take responsibility for your actions, embrace patience, foresight, and planning to succeed at it. Most importantly, taking responsibility comes with consequences—both positive and negative—and you have to accept them all.

On the opposite hand, a life built on material pleasure is unconscious and far from a purpose-driven one. A life of purpose will delay gratification in exchange for a long-term benefit and for you to be supremely patient with the environment and people. This level of living keeps you present. It's like living life after drinking an energy drink. Or having a strong cup of coffee, or that amazing feeling you get after exercising. It will seem like you are living your best life at its highest level. Keeping grounded and present is one of the biggest attributes of staying on your purpose.

Assume you have set a goal of starting a new business. You have chosen your launch date, and everything seems to be on track. However, your other obligations like family or a present-day job keep taking your attention away. Some level of sacrifice is needed to launch your business regardless of other responsibilities and make your best effort to ensure the launch sees the light of day. The real goal is ensuring that you fulfill your purpose, even if it means breaking it up into small tasks every day. As the day breaks, the accomplishment of each task takes you closer to that goal, which is your purpose of starting your company and leaving your job. It means everything to you. When you stay present, it helps you become more focused, thankful and passionate about what you currently have. When you are focused, distractions give way. That opens up the opportunity to reach your full potential—and it becomes possible because you're passionate with an immense amount of gratitude. It is simple to understand this possible scenario because you're living life based off your values and beliefs.

5

CRITICAL ELEMENTS OF PURPOSE

There are over 150 million blogs on the internet, but just a handful make a difference in our lives. Most people are content with average living, inauthentic lives, happy to stay in their comfort zones and not risk making a difference. The planet has a long list of unanswered problems—problems that many of us can fix. The questions we need to ask ourselves are: How can we solve a particular problem? Where would we be most useful? How can we serve others with the skill sets we have and with the chances we have? All of these questions will be answered if you understand the critical elements of living a purposeful life.

CONSISTENCY

You need to be consistent with yourself and display it in your behavior, no matter the person around. It will help you in a couple of ways: you'll be able to maintain focus and become adaptable while also being flexible. You'll face challenges with renewed vigor and overcome them. Purpose-driven individuals have unwavering consistency in their behaviors, and they are always who they are.

PSYCHOLOGICALLY FLEXIBLE

With a change in demand, opportunities spring up. These are the obstacles and life challenges that come in numbers. If you are flexible in your psychology, you experience fewer problems, unlike people who are not psychologically flexible.

EFFICIENT TIME AND ENERGY MANAGEMENT

Knowing when and how to deploy your time and resources is one of the best things that can happen to you. It is critical for your well-being and to live a life of purpose. A purpose-driven individual won't waste their time, actions and behaviors on trivial issues that do not align with their goals. They know what they want at every time and are constantly taking steps to achieve them. These critical elements are important ingredients to having a purpose-driven life, especially during times of uncertainty. These elements will help you stay focused on where you are going and the impact you want to make here on Earth. Without them, it is impossible to unpack and reach your purpose in life. Embrace them.

We'll now talk about the pursuit of multiple purposes. Frankly, on this planet, everyone has more than one purpose: We serve different purposes at different stages of our lives—and it could go through our different talents. I don't know who started it, and I hope I never figure it out because they have inflicted untold pain onto creative people. Some people admit they've gnashed their teeth and torn their clothing, trying to find out their main purpose in life. Let's debunk the lie that you were told. Repeat after me: "I've got more than one purpose. I'm on the planet to accomplish many things. Lots of things are giving me pleasure and purpose." You need to understand that having multipurpose is only good to a point—too many of them could derail you and move away from where you want to be.

The strategy here is that if you have one life purpose and some of the challenges and obstacles that you encounter along the way become too much to handle, you can switch your attention to the other purpose because they're all interdependent. So, then you can shift back and forth with your head in a similar direction. Having this mentality and approach is really good because it creates this lifestyle of being purposeful. It also increases the odds that you will achieve positive outcomes. Multiple purposes may not be good in the long run—or even switching purposes. It's all about time, attention and resources. The perfect approach would be to focus a bit on one and then switch to another as you encounter an obstacle. This way, you're headed in the right direction and can reap the benefits because it's all focused on one purpose.

6

WHY IT'S HARD TO FIND YOUR PURPOSE

I'm frequently asked, "Why can't I find my life purpose?" Over the years, I've heard a lot of people — whether they're people in therapy seeking to develop better lives or business executives striving to establish healthy leadership — say at some stage, they don't know what they're really here for. They are not necessarily religious or spiritually inclined, but they feel a longing for that "certain thing" that defines their lives and integrates them. At first glance, it seems very feasible to figure out your life purpose. But once you start the journey to uncovering your true self, you get stuck, and it becomes difficult. As I've mentioned above, you're going to encounter so many obstacles when you start looking for meaning and purpose in your life. It can take quite a while for you to figure out. Here are some typical issues that prevent many people from figuring out their life purpose:

SOCIETAL INFLUENCE

Society influences many things, including finding that purpose that seemed to have eluded you for a long while. Whether you like it or not, you have adopted the traditions and norms of society and culture. There are standards written and unwritten that society has set for judging people. Based on some of these standards, things are deemed popular or unpopular, and people are considered outcasts if they don't follow some of these traditional paths that society deems worthy.

All of this dates back to when we were kids but becomes really popular as we become adults. For instance, in high school, the popular kids are football players and athletes. Even the cheerleaders tend to be popular, as displayed in movies and the media. Young and impressionable students strive to be something they're not because they want to fit in. We're never really given permission to become ourselves. You give in to the influence of popular culture because you don't want to be considered an outcast. It all starts then, and unfortunately, carries on into adulthood.

So we go to college, strive to get that dream job, and also get married and live the "dream," only to find out that we've been living by someone else's rules. In many ways, this was my life until I found my purpose. As I mentioned before, I knew that life didn't have to be this way. It lacked meaning; it lacked direction and was never about work. I was stuck in an unhealthy relationship that was devoid of fulfillment. To make matters worse, I was spending money on things I did not need. Life felt so confusing. It didn't end there; I took to drinking a lot of alcohol, and I was paying less attention to my health. I kept drifting towards that path of destruction. On the outside, I was perfectly fine, doing the things the world wants to see. On the inside, it was a complete mess, and I was dying. I wanted to change but didn't know how.

If you're reading this right now and you've had a similar experience, just know there's a different path—that brings hope and fulfillment. In this book, I'll show you how you can turn your life around, even if you have given up on yourself. Yes, the days of uncertainty are upon you, and you can't seem to figure out your next line of action—let alone get past this week. There is light at the end of the tunnel. Others have been there, and today, they're out of the murky waters of confusion and charted a new path that gives fulfillment.

Some folks are very lucky to have discovered their purpose early on in life. Some people may seem to be born virtually shredding riffs on a guitar or deciphering the most sophisticated algorithms. It's a bit of a guessing game for the rest of us until we finally find something that just "clicks." Until then, we may feel lost or a bit useless. You may have felt lost at some point in your life—you were at a crossroad and utterly unsure where to turn. Because you have no sense of purpose, you feel stuck and keep asking, "Where do I go from here?" This is one of the unsettling sensations that one can experience. It is not surprising that people with an established sense of purpose seem to have higher self-esteem.

If you are still searching for a sense of purpose, here are critical questions for you: How do you love yourself if you've never been loved by others that are close to you? What if you were told that you are smart, beautiful, and worthy of greatness? Will that increase your self-worth? The answers to these questions will help move you closer or away to gain self-esteem for clearly defined purposes. The fact remains, the more you like yourself, the more confidence you gain. If you continue to love yourself, you'll become efficient and effective in each area of your life, gaining self-esteem in the process to live in purpose and be a top performer.

One of the most significant factors that stop you from finding your purpose is the idea that you don't get to follow your dreams. Unrealistic goals and dreams in the minds of other people prevent you from really living an authentic life. Let's say you wanted to be a designer or an architect or something in the creative field. However, growing up, you were made to believe that being creative wasn't a sensible, realistic career decision—then, society questions how you'll pay your bills and feed your family with such judgment. So you were forced into traditional and safe fields.

People who were not happy in their own life decisions are quick to place demands, boundaries and rules on what others should be doing with their own life. They are opposed to the idea that living your passion isn't a real-life achievement. They have designed a blueprint for your life—advising you on what's possible and what is not. When you have these constant shifts in mindset, your dreams start to disappear into thin air, and, at some point, you let go. In times of uncertainty, it's even worse because you're looking at what the news and the media is telling you. The people in your social feed are very harmful, and you can perceive their hate miles away. It would help if you had the mental clarity to stay true to your dreams. To achieve this goal, you need to cut through the noise and confusion that permeates your space.

It seems to be even worse as you get older. You tell yourself that you're too old to do new things, and you start placing limitations on your abilities, believing certain achievements are beyond your reach—even though you see young people achieving seemingly impossible feats. Then you look at the decisions you've made and realize it's impossible to live a more authentic life and live your purpose. You lose the hope to dream again and tell yourself that it's too late to reinvent yourself. For you, starting again is not part of the plan because of the many responsibilities and obligations that come with it. You may even look like a fool going that route. You're scared to be judged, and your dreams diminish even more. Just chill; you're not alone on this journey.

Listen, when you have a calling in whatever area, it will keep coming at you even if you refuse to admit it. Once you respond to it, you're responding to your purpose. Once you acknowledge the thing that's inside and call for it, then it gravitates towards you. That way, your dreams can start taking shape to become a reality. Another reason why it's hard to find your purpose is the fear of the dark side. The dark side is our most deep-seated inadequacies and secrets. The ones who embrace this and hold it in their hands are the most successful. It doesn't go away; you can only ignore it as many people do. It will always be a part of you unless you address it. Without adequately addressing it, it's going to hinder you from finding your full and real purpose. Until you get in touch with this side of yourself, your personality and past history, you won't find your purpose and rise to serve others. You're too busy trying to hide the dark side and pretend it's not there—but it certainly is.

No matter where you go or what you do, it's that thing that prevents you from fully manifesting your potential because you don't want other people to see it. Then you think it has stopped existing because you hide it. This is far from the truth; your deficiencies show up in your dark side. It's the embodiment of your failures, your flaws, and your insecurities. All of your selfish, wrong desires and deepest fears are encapsulated in your dark side. When you're on the path to finding yourself, you'll have to confront the dark side. Fear often pushes it down below to the point where you think that you can get by without embracing it.

Many people are oblivious to the fact that this flaw or fear helps us serve others and improve ourselves. Once you embrace this part of yourself, you'll show up and find your purpose. Nobody wants to reveal this side of themselves. It exposes you as a fraud or potentially opens you to criticism in your business and personal relationships. People may look at you differently. You're perfectly happy with this little secret and hope that nobody ever finds out. You're often afraid to see it manifest, and in your mind, you're like, "How has this become part of me? I hate myself for it."

But this all makes perfect sense; we all like to look at the bright side of ourselves, especially our comfort zones. It makes you feel complete, and you hope that you never have to encounter this dark side and reach your purpose. The dark side has another side to it (directly opposite)—the fear of questions that you don't necessarily have the answers to. It's so comfortable to know you have answers to these tricky questions, and it feels natural not to answer them. The hardest and the best part is when you embark on the path to finding your purpose or discovering answers to the questions you don't have the answers to. Some of these questions can really scare you, and that's why you don't necessarily want to answer them.

If you're the type who loves to control your image and behavior while in public, then it's only a matter of time to get used to what you know about yourself—that gives you a sense of control. You never want to put yourself in a situation where you don't know certain bits of information or knowledge about your personality. Imagine saying, "Oh my, I didn't know this about myself." It sounds terrifying, right? This is what stops you from finding your purpose. If you can overcome these obstacles, then finding your purpose is within your fingertips. But it's not such an easy feat—it's a constant battle within you to confront your deepest fears. If you decide to go all the way, you'll be much closer to making a bigger impact on your life and that of others.

Remember, when I mentioned earlier in the book about ending my long-term relationship, right before I started my nonprofit organization? I took a trip to Europe to get some coaching, and the events surrounding that journey brought up some deepest fears in my life. One of them happened in high school. I had got a scholarship to a wealthy private school in a suburb of New York. I kept it a secret because my family couldn't afford it. So for 4 years of high school, I pretended like I was a full-paying student at the school.

The second one was that we lived in a basement for most of my life in high school, then later on, a two-story family house—

where we lived on the top floor. My father was unemployed, and we struggled financially. Paying the bills was a problem. Bill collectors called so often, but my sister and I learned to avoid answering those calls. We got help from our local church and food pantries, and all of our clothes were secondhand, which we got from thrift stores. So, you can imagine how I felt when I would show up to school on a bus, while kids were getting dropped off in luxury cars.

My classmates would talk about their family vacations to far off and exotic destinations. They would display and talk about the kind of wealth they were exposed to. I couldn't make too many close friends because I was too ashamed of my family status—we were financially struggling and were just making it. I struggled with placing an identity to my personality, always pretending to be someone else. It was such a grueling experience to deal with all of that. As if that was not enough, being the only black male threw up other issues around class, race, and privilege that compounded the experience. It wasn't until I started to embrace who I was and that I was from a poor family (who struggled to make ends meet) that I began to gain clarity about my purpose. I was able to develop resilience and interpersonal skills that helped me become successful in life.

Even though my home life wasn't always secure and happy, I could relate to the youth in my organization, which gave me the leeway to embrace and adapt to different environments. I could talk to 15-year-old kids who lived in housing projects and turn around and relate to a wealthy donor in the same breath. The change in mindset played a crucial role in my fundraising and networking. My organization grew, and I was able to expand to other cities. The shame of having a poor background became the catalyst for accepting who I was and discovering my purpose here on earth. It was easy to relate with people struggling with an identity crisis because I had been through a similar journey.

7

HAPPINESS VS. FULFILLMENT

Ask an average person what they want out of life, and most will say they want to be happy. If you dig deeper into what that means, they'll say they want to feel good and comfortable. That sounds innocent on the surface, but pursuing happiness is indeed the cause of so many miseries here on earth. The notion that pleasure and contentment are the solutions to all the problems in life, and that you have everything you need once you acquire those states, is a misconception that may lead us astray. There's more to life than happiness.

Happiness is something that all humans can achieve. Happiness has a cult-like following to everyone who seems to believe it and thinks it's essential. However, happiness is subjective. It could be long-term or short-term. The worth could be as significant as whatever you can imagine in this world or so minutely like a tiny piece of paper. Everyone can relate to it since it's a more general term. Typical examples of what makes people happy are a good job, love, family, career, money, and health.

Fulfillment, on the other hand, is more personal; it's yours. Therefore, fulfillment is different for everyone. When you're passionate about something, you can experience fulfillment, such as a dream or a goal. Perhaps you're into volunteering, helping others, or maybe someone who loves activities that help promote your continuous growth and education. Maybe you're a community-minded person who loves being connected with a larger group of people than yourself. If you look at the difference between fulfillment and happiness, you'll realize fulfillment is long-lasting and more profound. Fulfillment is what you need to strive for.

The primary reason why you should embrace fulfillment is that it is unique and only for you. That is the thing that sets you apart from everyone else. Perhaps having the right diet and exercise routine fulfills you because you know it will improve your overall health. Your friends may not find workouts fulfilling—they're not seeking to live a healthy life. They probably want to look good in a bathing suit. To them, working out is not too exciting. Again, happiness is something that everyone feels the same about, but fulfillment gives you a sense of being and purpose. Happiness is more of a feeling, while fulfillment is something that you obtain after hard work and dedication by putting in time and effort. In many ways, fulfillment makes you a complete person.

In terms of timeframe, fulfillment is long-lasting, while happiness is fleeting and short-lived. Because of this, happiness isn't sustainable in the long haul. Do you know people who are happy all the time? A handful of people, I guess. Have you heard of the quote, "True success, true happiness lies in freedom and fulfillment?" It encapsulates what has been said earlier, and it makes more profound sense that true happiness finds its way in fulfillment. When you're fulfilled, it's perfectly fine not to be happy all the time. Fulfillment makes you accept things (the ones you have no power over) the way they are because you know there will be rough patches. It is permanently linked to your mind—and lives with you for a more extended period. For example, if being a yoga teacher makes you fulfilled, you'll put all your time, creativity, and energy into achieving that goal.

The rough patches will come— and this is no different from what others experience. You'll always be content in your heart and soul because you know that you're living your purpose. In happiness, you don't have a grasp of the time frame—how long or how short it will live. If something upsetting comes up in the news and the world, your happiness drifts away quicker than you can imagine, so it is not personal to you since it can go away so fast. Fulfillment isn't subject to the whims of incidents, feelings, or people—it belongs to you. You can keep it for as long as you want; no one can ever take it away.

Fulfillment gives meaning to success–not the other way around. Here's a quick example. Dave was a bright student in a family of smart children. He was raised to shadow his father's prosperous logistic business. Dave had a sound education from one of the best schools around, particularly enjoying medieval arts and philosophy. Then he got a call from his father to return to the business because they needed someone smart enough to run a product line. Even though Ted found moderate success in his job, his dreams had not been fulfilled. We often see this type of scenario play in our daily lives. We seek success, hoping it will bring fulfillment. Before we know it, we are asking for something else. What we fail to realize is that fulfillment gives meaning to success and not the other way round.

It's perfectly fine to be happy with your success. However, this feeling will eventually go away. Let's say you won a big project from a client for your business. It may feel like you're on top of the world at that moment, but this isn't something that fulfills you. Getting a big check or a contract is something that feels good. Does it give you fulfillment? If it's suddenly taken away, will you still be as excited as you were when you got the contract? If something makes you fulfilled, it will give you joy every single day. Happiness isn't sustainable. Fulfillment is, and that's what you should be aiming for.

If fulfillment is then the aim, you'll need to work hard—even though it is not fun. It will create a desire to achieve more. Otherwise, you'd cease to feel content. Your happiness may not come from listening to your favorite music, eating a slice of pizza, or going to the park. It may be as trivial as being around your favorite people. Even sleeping in and being lazy can create that happiness for you or spending time and hanging out with a friend. Those things can distract you from being fulfilled. In making fulfillment your priority, you'll get things done on time. You'll develop a sense of urgency that instigates you to act within an allotted time frame. At the end of the day, you'll feel more complete. You'll be content, knowing you did something meaningful with your day.

Staying in your comfort zone makes you happy, but it won't bring you fulfillment. You can take shortcuts to be happy, but there are no shortcuts to fulfillment. That's why going the extra mile can make you fulfilled. When you pursue fulfillment, you'll be eager to do new things. You'll become creative and seek new ways to get better. You'll step out of your comfort zone, taking the bull by the horn to confront challenges. You'll completely surprise yourself. If you find fulfillment in your job or business, you'll never dread Monday mornings, and you won't even think about working during the weekends or evenings, especially if you're happy with the result and how it makes you feel at the end of the day. Why are some people so passionate about their job? It is simple—they found fulfillment.

Happiness is a one-time feeling. Think of a single color in a rainbow, even though the rainbow is made up of so many different colors. Happiness includes passion, drive, failure, grief, emotion. All of these must happen for fulfillment to take place. That's what makes it so unique. There's nothing wrong with being happy. The question is, would you like to live life with only one color or through all of the different colors to get what you want. To make progress, you must provide an answer to this question. There are times when you're not happy, but overall, you are fulfilled.

For example, let's say that you are an attorney who works with small businesses and entrepreneurs. You work long hours, but you're not necessarily happy working there. There are some problematic clients and cases under your purview. Some days, you have to deal with frustration, anger, and delays. However, you're at peace with yourself because each of your successes is an affirmation that you're doing what completes you. When you're writing a contract that seals up a business deal, you have provided a livelihood for the company's employees and meaningful service to their customers. And you feel complete too—it's your purpose because you do it with love, commitment, and passion. For a lot of people, this feeling isn't enough to keep them going. They're always looking for ways to get better when they're fulfilled. An essential element of life is happiness. However, you can only achieve that when you live a fulfilled life.

8

AVOIDING FALSE PURPOSE

I f you look around, you'll see that most people have the same dream. When you look a little deeper, you'll realize that everybody has the same "purpose" when they mention it to you. It's usually around making a certain amount of money, traveling around the world or building a family. They all sound familiar because your friends and family constantly feed you with these words for years, and now it's stuck in your head. Then people tend to conflate these with other platitudes like "help other people" or "be a good human" as if these are the sole purpose of humanity.

Did you ever think about the role you have in determining your life purpose? Were you ever consulted along the way, or was it decided for you? Your teachers and mentors inadvertently made the decision for you, and you accepted it hook, line, and sinker. In your ignorance, you thought it was only natural to pursue these life purposes. You had no idea they were conditioned messages and suggestions. You fell for it, thinking they were better life choices. They even gave you instructions to follow to determine your life's path. When you take a moment to ponder over these supposed life decisions and how they have affected your life, you discover they do not align with you—they were all forced on you by someone else.

It's easy to think these false purposes are meant for you and your life. It could have been influenced by society, your family, or your colleagues. All of these factors, one way or the other, created this false purpose—and made you believe it was yours. However, it's not at all. There is an array of "find/live/be" your purpose messages around the internet today. There may be a trap in just using the word "purpose" to describe your direction, reason, or aim in life. When you're just seeking "purpose," it leaves you open to living someone else's purpose and making it yours. I refer to that as "a phony purpose."

I suggest that purpose needs a qualifier like the word "authentic." Authentic means not false or copied; genuine; real. If untied from results such as a degree, resume-boosters, dream graduate school, friends, family, advisors, travel, goals of profit, what would be your reason for existence? Your personal or organizational *authentic purpose* lies underneath all these inconsistent results. Your most significant competitive advantage is your authentic purpose. That is why you live in the world as an individual or organization, independent of others. You must first recognize and understand the "phony" purpose that you're chasing in life before uncovering and unleashing your authentic purpose. How do you recognize this "phony" or false purpose? The best way to recognize a false purpose is that it doesn't feel right; it's not your calling. A lot of times, it's been imposed on you by others. It could have been a thought or an idea or suggestion—but it's never yours. Those who live with purpose in their life often say purpose isn't related to money or your career. It's about being your true and authentic self. This is the part of you that is often hidden from the public until you discover it.

It is common practice for society or family to impose certain career choices or ways of life on people. You never get to experience your true self. Instead, you curl back into your shell, waiting for the right time. If you went to college, your family expected you to get a good degree. Your family dictates your course of study—be it a creative course or some other subjects. Let's say you live on the east coast, but your dream was to always live in California. You never really had the opportunity to live outside of your small town or experience a different life. So, you stayed close to home with mountains of regrets to deal with. These reasons are keen to make you take on a false purpose. You never signed up for this kind of life—it was forced on you by others because you needed to fulfill certain expectations.

This happens all the time in life. Others' demands and needs come before yours, and next thing you know, you feel obligated to keep certain friendships, activities, traditions, and customs because well, it's something you do. It's who you are. In a bigger way, people subconsciously manipulate you into believing that the "phony" or false purpose is your real purpose.

False purpose can cripple your ability to advance in life. You don't have to embrace this way of life. You can live a more purposeful life if you choose to by steering clear of false purpose (I usually call it "phony" purpose). It can lead you astray into doing things you never planned. It can mess with your self-esteem and confidence. When the dust settles, you'll be full of regrets in having made bad life choices. No one has found fulfillment living that kind of life.

I've experienced something like this. I went through depression, and I was constantly saying, "This can't be life! There has to be more to it." The modern conveniences within your house or apartment give you joy when you look at them—your gym membership, your car, etc.—even your job. In times of uncertainty, you lose everything, and it all comes crashing down. Then you realize that the life you had is something you don't want any more. Before now, it was about comparing yourself to others and the possessions and status they've attained in their lives and careers. Like me, you may be asking questions like, "What else haven't I done? How am I different from them? How is my life more fulfilling than theirs? Did I work my butt off to be just like others?"

One question that set it off for me and anybody that needs to get out of any unfavorable situation is, "If I could do anything in the world right now (to change my situation), what would that be?" I had closed down my company because of the economic downturn and lost a lot of clients. I had a lot on my mind at that time. To make matters worse, I was severely hit financially and on the verge of breaking up a 7-year relationship after a big fight with my fiancée.

My world was crashing down right before my eyes. I cried my eyes out every day in the wee hours of the night. The incidents kept replaying in my head—how my life deflated and lost meaning. Imagine someone you loved so dearly and has always been there when you need her most. Suddenly, she slipped through your fingers and drifted miles away, never to return. Then that question resonated through my mind: If I could do anything in the world right now to change my situation, what would that be?

I decided to buy a ticket to British Columbia and visit my uncle and also go snowboarding. That trip was my watershed moment. The whole idea of my nonprofit organization came to bear—from asking critical questions and then following my heart. I discovered snowboarding, and then my purpose followed suit. To simplify the answer: I needed to go snowboarding to discover my nonprofit initiative—which opened the door to self-discovery and purpose. When you stay away from your false purpose and find meaning in life, you need to be true to yourself and follow what your heart is telling you. I couldn't be happier that I followed my heart and booked the ticket to go to Canada for snowboarding. It was an eye-opening experience.

With your heart saying something, listen and pay close attention to it. Often, the naysayers are closer than you think, and you don't have to listen to them. I adopt a rule—never take advice from people that have done less than you. When you find your real purpose, it is something that you want, something that you thought of yourself or got inspiration from others. If you refuse to do it, you'll feel like a piece of your soul is missing. I hate to sound so dramatic, but before I started my nonprofit, it was just an idea (that seemingly had no weight), but I kept talking about it with everybody that cared to listen. I was so passionate about it that I even discussed it with my coworkers back then.

I knew there were going to be a lot of regrets if I didn't make a move. So I took the plunge, regardless of what the outcome would be. Today, I can say I'm glad I did. That's the beauty of finding your purpose and being true to yourself. It's not about pushing yourself to do it; it's about attracting the forces around to key into that burning desire to fulfill your life purpose. You'll naturally have the energy to do it and realize that it lights you up. Even when things are pretty tough, you'll be energized to continue on this path. When you steer clear of false purpose, you become fearless in your approach. Not even society, friends and family can dictate for you again. You know you're doing this for yourself—and you're not accountable to anyone.

If you want to stay away from false purpose, you'll have to listen to yourself. You have to ignore what everyone says. Spend time getting to know yourself and learn about you. In doing so, you'll understand what drives and motivates you. If you care enough about yourself, do the work to find things that excite you, and during this process, it's essential to stay fearless. Don't be afraid to fail, and even if you fail, embrace it whole-heartedly. Feeling very vulnerable and making mistakes or being rejected is part of this process. People that are close to you may be disappointed by your actions. Others will say they don't know anymore. But none of that matters. During this process, a critical question is, "How do I know that I'm not pursuing a false purpose?" The answer is simple: if you're feeling unfulfilled, then you may very well have a false purpose.

When following your real purpose, you're inspired every single day; you'll discover new things in the process and be happy to go down the proverbial rabbit hole and stay there as long as you want. The false purpose will always rear its ugly heads early. It would help if you defined your purpose to stay away from false purpose. When you do that in advance, regrets will remain far from you. Now you have to gain clarity. Then finding your real purpose becomes an easier task. Ultimately, what matters is fulfillment. Don't let anyone choose the path you must follow. They may have their expectations, but it may not necessarily align with yours.

> *"People take different roads seeking fulfillment and happiness. Just because they're not on your road doesn't mean they've gotten lost."*
> —Dalai Lama

People's idea of fulfillment doesn't have to be yours. So quit living by other people's terms and start living by your terms. What matters is your life purpose. Antoinette Foy says, "The core of your true self is never lost. Let go of all the pretending." The philosophy behind this concept is to let yourself in. Once you allow that to happen, you won't even need to find yourself. Your true self will appear in front of you. This is the ultimate way to find your real purpose.

9

THE IMPORTANCE OF DEFINING YOUR LIFE PURPOSE

"There's no greater gift than to honor your life's calling. It's why you were born. And how you become most truly alive."
 – Oprah Winfrey

When you find your life's purpose, it'll help you achieve new levels on your life journey. Before you do that, you need to clearly define the things that happen around you and the logical steps to achieve them. In taking this step-by-step approach, you'll find what you need to do. For example, when cooking a recipe, you have to follow a step-by-step approach for a tasty and delicious meal. So, it's only logical to define your purpose before you go out and find it.

Frederick Buchner once said, "Purpose is the place where your deep gladness meets the world's needs." Before you go about serving the world, you need to define this place; you can't get to this place without first defining it. When you find your purpose, you get direction. It leads you towards the ultimate goal. If you must achieve anything in life, you have to be very clear about it. And that's why successful people believe winning comes from having a purpose. But there must be a strong desire to achieve it. If you lack direction, you will go around in circles. It's like going on a journey—there must be directions and also a destination. Without both, then your journey is baseless.

In the same vein, if you have no definition, you can't get to your purpose. For you to find purpose, you need to know exactly where you're going. Through this process, you'll have to dig deep into yourself, and by asking the "why," you'll uncover new questions and learn new things about yourself.

None of this is easy, though. When you start the process, you'll be confused. As I said above, so many new questions will pop up that you don't have answers to. Know for sure, the doubts and confusion will go away. You'll gain clarity about your goals and how to reach them.

Successful people know what they want and why they want it. They have direction, and most importantly, they know what success means. They're aware of "why" they need to be successful. Once the definition occurs, everything you do will be consistent with your goals. All of your actions, relationships, thoughts, and tasks will bring you closer to your aims and your purpose. The first step is to know your "WHY." When you grasp the "WHY," it's going to help you filter out a lot of your actions—or maybe distractions. You are going to be able to prioritize the unimportant versus the essential and what you need to do. The scale will fall off your eyes (so to speak), and you'll understand what and who to cut out during the process. We'll discuss your "WHY" in part 2.

The best part of knowing your purpose is that it keeps distractions far away from you. When you're on your path to finding your purpose, shiny object syndrome will come knocking at your door, and it's almost designed to get you sidetracked. Here is what you need to know. Your lifetime consists of days, hours, and minutes. Although it doesn't seem like much for a minute or ten, the idea that you could waste a few minutes is the biggest, fattest lie you'll ever tell yourself. Life is fast, time flies, and no one will wait for you or have pity on you because you stayed behind, absorbed by distractions and useless clutter. If you're not careful, your life will get ruined even before you realize it.

Hundreds of decoys move to the front seat of your life, and collectively, they will take over the steering wheel if you encourage them. They always promise excellent results and benefits, but what they do is just prevent you from doing important things and achieving your major goals. When you know your purpose in life, all the decoys (distractions) will stay far away from you because you can identify them when they come close. It is important you have a clear sense of where you're headed. If you wake up without a plan and one day decide to do anything, it will be hard to succeed. On the other hand, if you have no plan and keep moving like a person without direction, purpose is lost to the wind, and you'll remain clueless on how to navigate your way.

As an example, you may believe that your life is to help people overcome trauma and loss in their life. Unless you know how you can get there, it is a mere dream, and it will remain elusive as long as you lack the perfect plan. You might get distracted by people and world events. They may tell you that that's an unworthy life purpose or that there are enough people out there doing the same thing that you want to do. Then you get deflated and lose hope. At this stage, if your purpose isn't well-defined, it will get distracted and truncated by someone else's myopic view about your life.

You get distracted by what is happening on social media, and then you follow the bandwagon—abandoning what you originally planned with your life. Unknown to you, you're headed down a steep cliff. When you find your purpose, you find the right path. You'll ask critical questions, such as why you want to serve others and what drives you to do so. "Why must this be my purpose and not something else?" "What are the challenges in my life that I overcame? How can I help other people overcome challenges as well? When you provide answers to all these questions, you get a better idea and a clear sense of purpose, and then your path will become much clearer. After you define your purpose, you'll take more risks regardless of the magnitude. You'll be open to new or unconventional things and impact others in a way that aligns with your purpose.

Organization is one of the attributes that come with a self-defined purpose. Instead of thinking about what to do next, you have it all planned out— and so clear. On the other side of the divide, confusion is the order of the day. You can't place your finger on what to do next. Your thoughts are always racing with so many things going through your mind. And you'll be like, "I think I know my purpose, but where do I start?"

I can't overstate the importance of thinking through this process—you need time to do this. You need to be in the best frame of mind and easy on yourself to know what to do and what needs to get done. It's not such a hard nut to crack. You can decide to write down what needs to be done. If you have a well-designed purpose, then have a day-to-day plan on how to achieve it. This is not cast in stone; other people may decide to go through a different route. For some, they need to think about the process of what's next when they eventually find their purpose. Others have aha moments and are always inspired to come up with a master plan right off the bat. As soon as you find your inspiration and you have your plan, start your journey.

Think of it as a bike ride. To start the ride, you need a bike first. Then you need a clear idea of your destination and why you are going there. Without these facts, it's going to be hard to start. When your thoughts are organized, you won't have any confusion or even distractions that often mar this process. Milne explains this well when he says, "Organization is what you do before you do something." He further says that you do this so that everything doesn't get mixed up. This makes perfect sense because if all of your thoughts and plans are mixed up, a lot of disarrays impede your progress, and confusion sets in. Finding your purpose means sticking to a single plan, which leads you to the ultimate goal—your purpose.

This is probably one of the fun parts of finding your purpose. When you decide to go on this path, a lot of experimentation emerge, and you'll have fun in this process. Explore and learn new things about yourself. When you're defining what's important to you, what kind of values you want and how it relates to your life, you'll start to see your true self. If you set out to find your purpose, you may derail. This can completely change your original purpose. If you have already experimented, explored and defined, it will be worthwhile to learn more about yourself, and you can see your passions and talents and your hidden interest. You may even find things that surprise you. Then look deep into yourself to find your calling, your reason for being and your drive.

UNCOVERING YOUR PASSION

Discovering what you love and are passionate about is not as challenging as society makes it seem. Passion isn't reserved for a select few —it's something everybody can attain with the right attitude. Passion is supposed to be fun, so take the time to explore what it brings to your life. Instead of calling yourself hopeless, start by visualizing unlimited potential and possibilities. The truth is, you're only limited to doing what you love by your lack of imagination, references, and role models. Here are some simple and straightforward tips that will help you discover your purpose and meaning and break out of this cycle of uncertainty and lack of passion:

GIVE YOURSELF THE OPPORTUNITIES

Being passionate about something isn't any magical experience —it's a simple process of finding that thing you love doing and would do over and again. Passion is the force that keeps us going, that fills us with joy, enthusiasm and anticipation. Passion is a strong force to accomplish anything you set your mind to and reach the maximum extent possible in work and life. Passion is ultimately the driving force behind success and happiness, which enables us all to live better lives. Little wonder, Oprah Winfrey put it as "Passion is energy. Feel the power that comes from focusing on what excites you." A lot of times, the reason why you aren't doing what you love is you don't believe you deserve to be passionate about what you do.

Everyone has the right to be passionate about their life and pursuits. One of the most freeing and liberating feelings is to wake up excited about your life, and you have every right to do so. Just because others are not excited about their lives doesn't mean you shouldn't. When you open your mind and pursue what you do passionately, you'll be able to help others do the same. To achieve this, there has to be a change of mindset, and you have to know what you want to do with your life. Once you shift your mindset to create an identity of one who is filled with passion and purpose, then attaining fulfillment in what you do will feel like a breeze

EXPLORE, EXPLORE AND EXPLORE!

There's a belief that there's at least one true passion for everyone, and everything else is not worth the focus of our effort. It's like an all-or-nothing mindset. However, the danger with this approach is that it makes you miss out on opportunities to live more passionately. You'll have to understand the full scope of possibilities as it relates to fulfillment and enjoyment of what you do and spend your time doing. One perspective of the spectrum is the work that you hate and can't do under any circumstance. On the flip side is the work you love, and just the sheer thought of it gives you so much hope, excitement and energy. In between both of these possibilities are things that take your time, and you may not like them—a tedious job or challenging task.

The best thing you can do is keep moving forward in the direction that makes you feel so alive. When you pursue what you love, a lot of options and opportunities will spring up for you to live your life purpose. The more aggressive and passionate you are, the more it excites you, and the clearer you become at knowing what you want and what you don't want. Know for sure that everything else is going to drain your energy and distract you from your desired goal. Being passionate about what you do will not come out of the blue—it grows over time. You will like your work and then grow into being passionate about it. So don't spend a lot of time and energy with the mindset that you hate working, let alone working to find your passion. You will also turn away from the things that you could potentially love, and it can blind you.

One of my mentors said you should do what you love. I have always loved snowboarding, and then my passion grew for the sport. I was willing to go the extra mile to ensure I impact using snowboarding as a means. I would get on bus trips or borrow people's cars. I would get a little amount of sleep and save any money I could lay my hands on to go snowboarding. I felt lightweight and free when I embarked on this activity. I felt like I could do anything I set my mind to. I was in a zone replete with unlimited possibilities. I stayed utterly present to what was in front of me. It was like nothing else in the world mattered. With that motivation and feeling, my nonprofit was on the verge of seeing the light of day. Then I shared my love for snowboarding with young kids of color and from low-income backgrounds. I love working with my organization—their challenges are in purpose with helping other people. So, it's not inconceivable to create work and find purpose based on that, and I'm proof of it.

LOOK CLOSELY AT WHAT YOU'RE DOING

There are so many opportunities right in front of us. We tend to look at the traditional ways people make a living and do not think that you can make a living doing what you love to do. But it's as simple as doing this: Reframe your mindset and think about your perspective and change it. You'll realize how fascinating and exciting things you're doing currently are—but you never knew until now.

The ways to put your passion to good use, making money and finding purpose are numerous. It feels very natural when I tell people I run a nonprofit organization—they're fascinated by it, and they wondered how I could realize such a goal. The thing with people is that they don't think they can make a career off what they're passionate about. It is possible, and all you need to do is reframe your mind and aim it at serving a community. By serving people, there's always a market where people run to for solutions to their problem.

I never thought there would be plenty of snowboarders, skateboarders and surfers who love to share their stories of how the sports have changed their lives. But it was a big need that needed to be filled—and my organization was there to meet it all.

So many kids never had an interest in traditional sport or after school programs. Even the programs to introduce them to new environments and experiences were non-existent. Fortunately, my organization was there to fill the gap; we attracted so many kids interested in alternative activities. It was a perfect match as other adults jumped on the opportunity to share their life experiences with the kids. Just like others, I was so excited to share my passion and help kids find theirs too. I have been on this career path for 15 years, and there's no plan of stopping any time soon.

QUESTION YOURSELF

The most overlooked steps we fail to take is asking ourselves critical questions. It is easy; all you need is to let go of other activities and look inwards. It would help if you had time to do this.

We let trivial things take precedence over other things that excite us. To search out yourself, set aside quality time to figure out what makes you excited. Here are some questions that could help you discover your passion and purpose:

- What would you enjoy doing, even if you won't get paid for it?
- Do you have any gifts or skills that you can share with the world?
- In your life, when did you feel most creative?
- What comes naturally to you?
- What are your most successful accomplishments?
- These questions are designed to unveil the parts of your subconscious mind and open up what you're passionate about.

ALWAYS TEST YOUR PASSION

To fully commit to your passion, taking yourself down a particular path and start spending money, you need to test it to see if it aligns with your life (I call it the credibility test). You can do this by taking courses and watching videos online, reading interviews of people who have similar passions and reaching out to people that might be of help on this journey. By testing your passion, you'll understand whether it is real or it's just a fleeting idea with no real possibilities of applying it to your life. After you find your passion, start embracing it right away. It would be best if you immersed yourself in it. Start creating actions to embody this path instead of half committing to it. You may tick all of the boxes when it comes to happiness in your job, family, and other things, yet you're unfulfilled? If you feel that something is missing and the feeling refuses to go away, then that missing piece could be your purpose.

This is where you need to sit down and reevaluate your life. By asking critical questions as outlined above and then looking inwards, you'll find the answers. No one knows you better than you know yourself. So only you can fix the puzzle to your life and then find that purpose. When you find it, nurture and grow it. And when you accomplish that, you've added so much meaning to your life.

FIND WHAT EXCITES YOU

Your purpose should excite you. If your job, relationships and hobbies don't, they're not your passion. Are you continually looking at the clock, hoping that what you're doing ends as quickly as possible? Or do you dread getting up in the morning to go to work? All of us have some talent; we have something inside of us that makes us unique and different. It would help if you did everything in your power to find that thing. Just know that you won't be good at it the first time you give it a shot. You can't expect to be perfect, even if it's your talent. You'll have to learn it. To perfect it, get a mentor, so it can be something that you own and is ultimately yours. Even the best music artists and creative people have to practice regularly to be the best in their craft.

How do you know what your talent or your special gift is? As tough as the question seems, it's a no brainer; it usually comes very easily to you. It could also be something that you worked hard in the past to overcome, and now people come to you to help them overcome it too. It could be designing or problem-solving or collaborating with people or new ideas for businesses. If you enjoy doing any of these, this could be your true calling. If it's always been easy for you to draw or write or even do some public speaking, then look in that direction—especially if it comes so natural to you, and you can do it with your eyes closed. These are the clues that tell you where your real passion lies, but you have to find a path to channel it.

Have you ever had the strange feeling that you already know how to do something you're doing for the first time? You need to dig deep and look for that feeling. Steve Jobs has the best advice in this regard. According to him, you have to trust in something in your life. It could be gut, destiny, life, karma, or whatever. He says this approach makes a lot of difference in your life.

ASK YOURSELF WHY

"Why" is one of the most important questions you can ever ask yourself? Ask yourself why you want to do something or why not? When you're asking the "why" question, it helps cut through the distraction to help you focus on having clarity on your purpose. If you know the reason why you do certain things, you will be able to find your purpose with ease. Look inwards and think about the reasons why you have your current job. Perhaps you're on this career path because you earn a fat salary. Maybe you're in this career because of family obligations. You are a doctor because your mother was a doctor, or it could be something that you stumbled into by accident. Suppose these reasons justify the "why," then you're not living your life purpose. Your why and your answer should be about fulfillment and contentment. If it's not in line with your purpose, then reconsider what you're doing. If you wanted to be a musician and want to pursue it as a career, you need to ask yourself, "Why do I want to be a musician?" If the voice inside you tells you it's about meaning and fulfillment, you're on the right path, and that path will take you on to your purpose.

If you're doing something out of fear or by obligation, you need to let it go and abandon it because that's not your purpose. Once you figure out why you need to act quickly, start doing it.

The more you take action on your way, the more things become clear to you. Instead of overthinking whether something is going to work out or not, you should start doing—it doesn't have to come out perfectly the first time. Assume you're experimenting. If it's a new business, don't think about making money; instead, think about adding value and getting results for people. If it's a creative endeavor, experiment with getting feedback and putting out as much work as possible to find your voice. Take small actionable steps every day towards your calling. Once you start this path, discouraging words will start flying everywhere. These words may come from friends, family or co-workers, so don't pay attention to words that don't serve you.

"No matter how hard the battle gets or no matter how many people DON'T believe in your dream, never give up!"
-Eric Thomas

Don't see the discouraging words; see your goals; see your passion. They are all distractions to get you off track. The questions will start pouring in—and in numbers too. They're threatened by your progress and want to leave feedback. These days, it comes in the form of a text message or a comment on a post on social media. Trust me, I've been there; you have to ignore them. People who blatantly tell you that they don't like what you do, even as you're just starting, are the ones to ignore the most. Don't allow anyone to make you feel less of yourself, your passion, or purpose.

With that said, you need to realize that you're the only one that can stop yourself from making progress. You'll have a lot of self-doubts; you will question your purpose and why it has to be so. At this juncture, you need to trust that you're making the right decision regardless of what you are confronted with.

EXPLORE YOUR OPTIONS AND EXPAND YOUR TENTACLES

Why do people get stuck? Their minds are fixated on one thing they were supposed to do. When it does not happen for them, they lose hope, and confusion sets in. Going by that approach, you may waste a lot of time looking for the wrong thing, and when you find it, you'll realize it wasn't meant for you. What a time-waster. Why would you explore one thing when you can make do with so much more? Do you realize that being limited to one thing can stop you from reaching your full potential? For instance, you may be a creative person who likes to design, take photographs, and build with your hands. You may enjoy every aspect of the job and be equally good at them. To even think you have a passion for them makes it more interesting. Being a creative carries so much weight and meaning.

Stop thinking that you have to fulfill only one purpose when you could be doing so much more with your passions. Don't hesitate to jump in and explore new things; spread your tentacles. Don't turn off the unknown or your worst fears—any of those could be your calling. Follow your passions to make them more purposeful. In living a more passionate life, you become more purposeful. When you lack passion in life, seek your purpose; that's a perfect time. This makes you feel more disconnected to fix the lack; you need to inject more passion into your life. Look for people who inspire you to help you find your passion. For instance, if an entrepreneur or thought leader inspires you, ask questions about how they overcame this struggle and made their lives more meaningful.

LET YOUR DOUBTS EXPRESS THEMSELVES—NEVER SUPPRESS THEM

Your doubts are part of the process of helping you realize your purpose. You'll be doing yourself a great disservice by suppressing your doubts—they need to express themselves. You have the ideas, the courage, and beliefs to live the life you want. You may still not have any piece of the puzzle. The blueprint or plan may still be far from perfect. Maybe you haven't even activated your dreams. Yet this thing called life — and doing it on your terms — isn't as hard as we make it seem. It's not the action of others that makes things complicated. It is ourselves. It is called doubt, and it can cripple the best of us — even those of us who are inspired, self-conscious, and full of hopes and positive energy. Even though doubt creates uncertainty about which decision is going to be best for you, it's not a bad thing to experience it.

If you come to terms with your doubts when they surface, you're still making some progress. Ignoring them will make your life a mess. If you're having doubts about your current work and think you'd be better in another field, take some time to think about the best option. When you're done, and you think that you've found your purpose but still have some level of doubt, don't submerge it—let it flow to the surface. If you don't, you'll be stuck in another false purpose. When searching for your purpose, you're going to be riddled with ambiguities, fear, and doubts. It's important to note that the joy you derive when you finally find your purpose matters. You'll be one step closer with this mindset.

PART II
10 WAYS TO FIND MEANING & PURPOSE

PREFACE

This section of the book is the good stuff. The meat of the book that will reveal ten different ways to find your purpose and meaning in life. If you're stuck, you can use any combinations of these current practices to find your purpose. I've used every single one of them to stay motivated and on course with my purpose—it's a never-ending process. The first method, finding your WHY is probably the most important. It sets the tone and the energy around the process of finding your purpose.

There are a couple of foundational elements, like gratitude and meditation, as they require little commitment, but you can add more as you continue down the path. As you create more time and gain confidence, you can start embarking on pursuing your passions, volunteering, building networks, and doing social challenges. The next level is starting a side hustle, forming a mastermind, and investing in mentoring and coaching.

I'm excited for you to embark on this path. Now that we have set a solid foundation for understanding your purpose and why it's important to have one, I'm going to teach you how to find and have it be a part of your life. I'm still learning every day about my purpose, and it keeps getting more and more refined. Life purpose secrets are a way of life, and I'm thrilled to share them with you.

CREATING YOUR WHY STATEMENT

I recommend that the first thing you do is create a WHY statement. This will set the tone and path to finding your purpose. It will help you decide what you want from your life and be the driving force behind your goals. If you set goals that do not align with your personal WHY statement, I doubt if you will ever achieve them. Having an individual WHY statement for every goal that you set is necessary because you can make these specific to each of them. As long as the goal WHY statements all fit your overall personal WHY statement, then you're in line.

Ideally, your WHY statement should be the most effective way to express your real purpose in life. It needs to be clear and precise, but it should also be clear to others that you want to share it with. In this section, we will focus on your personal WHY statement. Here are the four recommended ideals for a WHY statement:

1. Your WHY statement is clear and straightforward.
2. Your WHY statement is actionable.
3. Your WHY statement is focused on the contribution you will make to others.

4. Your WHY statement is expressed in a positive way
   that resonates with you.

How long should your WHY statement be? The shorter, the better, but it needs to encapsulate the four ideas above, so it will be as long as it needs to be. Some people can write their WHY statement in one sentence – yours may be more than this. It doesn't matter. So I have a strategy for creating my statements, and it's a compelling way to own your story and where you are currently in life. This type of process will give a ton of reflection on how far you've come and where you need to be. It's the proverbial road map for being able to create your purpose in life.

The first step is to write down and describe yourself as accurately as possible and what life is like for you right now. The next thing to do is write down 3 to 7 milestones in your life that deeply impacted you. These milestones have shaped your life and made you who you are today. Once you identify the specific milestone, you'll describe what it was. Indicate whether it was positive or negative. Also, know whether it had an impact on your life and what it did for you. Lastly, I want you to write down how you feel emotionally when you are going through it and describe these specific emotions and feelings during that time.

Here's how it looks:

- Milestone #1: (Name)
- What was it: (describe)
- Positive or Negative:
- What impact did it have on your life?
- How did you feel when it was happening?

The next thing to do is describe the common thread between them. Write down in bullet points the common themes you see in every single one of those milestones. Now it's time to start summarizing the common threads in the form of the example below. It was recommended by well-known author, Simon Sinek. And you can start using the format for your WHY statement:

To _____ So That_____.

Here's an example of my WHY Statement:

FIRST MILESTONE:

Getting a scholarship to a private high school

- **What was it?** A wealthy man decided to give me a scholarship. My family couldn't afford to send me to the school. As a result, it changed my life.
- **Positive or Negative?** Positive
- **What impact did it have on your life?** It exposed me to a different network of people, gave me opportunities, interpersonal and social skills, and I learned how to network with wealthy people. My peer network was successful.
- **How did you feel when it happened?** I felt confused like a fish out of the water, uncomfortable, and ashamed because my family couldn't afford the school; I felt like I was hiding my TRUE identity.

SECOND MILESTONE:

Going to Stony Brook University

- **What was it?** A friend's family friend was the director of the admission, and she offered me and my friends an admission. Our grades didn't qualify us, but we made it to the school through her influence.

- **Positive or Negative?** Positive
- **What impact did it have on your life?** I got some excellent college roommates who motivated me to get an internship. I started taking classes to prepare me for success. That internship, coupled with my skills, got me a career in marketing and led to my first business at 24 years old.
- **How did you feel when it happened?** Overwhelmed but grateful to be given an opportunity. I didn't want to waste it.

THIRD MILESTONE:

Depression & Anxiety after 9/11

- **What was it?** After 9/11, I got a lot of anxiety and depression. I drank a lot, took up unhealthy behaviors, and felt lost.
- **Positive or Negative?** Negative
- **What impact did it have on your life?** I had several anxiety attacks, and I was depressed. I went searching for something different. That's where I discovered mentoring. I started mentoring kids, and I was mentored too. I would mentor a kid for 1 hour a week, setting aside all distractions. I learned to discover and pursue the things that I love, one of which was snowboarding. It was on a snowboarding trip that I realized I wanted to snowboard with my mentee. That was how the idea of STOKED was born.
- **How did you feel when it happened?** I felt like I was in constant transition. It was a lot. I felt I was

learning a lot about myself. I didn't know I could cry so much!

WHAT WAS THE COMMON THREAD IN ALL OF THEM?

- I was given a chance from school to opportunities.
- I had mentors.
- At my lowest point, the best part of my life was mentoring and helping kids.
- I was successful, and I wanted more meaning in life.
- I've impacted a lot of people through entrepreneurship and giving back.

MY WHY SUMMARIZED:

- To pass on the skills, opportunities, and experiences that I had in my life so purpose-driven entrepreneurs can build businesses that impact future generations.

You can use your WHY statement for motivation. What makes some people happy to go to work every day when others can't wait for the workday to end? What decides whether you derive deep fulfillment from your job or see it as a way to pay the bills? What motivates people to take action or only to do what they're assigned? The WHY. No matter what path you decide to take in life, there will be times when you do not feel like doing something that you know you should do. Your head is not in the game for some reason, and you find it difficult to focus and get things done.

With a strong and compelling WHY statement, you can quickly motivate yourself and get back on track. We recommend that you read your WHY statement out loud every morning immediately when you get out of bed. This will energize you and put you in the best possible state to meet the day's challenges. Keep a copy of your WHY statement with you—wherever you go. If you are feeling deflated for whatever reason at any time of the day, you can read your WHY statement and motivate yourself to push forward.

Sometimes, being inspired to do something and having good willpower is not enough for you to see it through to the end. So use your WHY statement to give you that motivational boost that will get you over the line. If you are truly committed to your personal WHY statement, you should have no problem sharing it with other people. Share it with your employer, family members, close friends, and anyone important to you.

Explain to them that you have found your WHY in life. This is how you will live your life from now on. By doing this, you add extra accountability to conforming to your WHY statement. If you need to explain it in more detail to some people, then be sure to do that. It is essential that everyone fully understands. So should you share your WHY statement with everyone you know? Well, it's your call. If you know that you will receive a negative reaction from some people, you may choose not to share it with them. You have to assess whether the people you choose to share your WHY statement with will provide extra accountability and motivation for you.

In all honesty, you should be proud of your WHY statement and the person that you want to become. It doesn't matter if some people think that you're crazy or that you won't live up to it. There will always be negative people in the world, so you need to accept this and deal with it. So my advice is to be very proud of your WHY statement and tell everyone about it!

If you have set goals that you were not committed to in the

past and either failed to achieve them or just gave up on them, it's time for a change. Your WHY statement will help you set the right goals. This is because you now have total clarity about where your life is going. Without this clarity, it will always be a challenge to set goals that you are truly committed to and inspired you. With the clarity through your WHY statement, you can then set new goals that will align with it. You know what you want to do and the impact you want to make, so start working on how you will achieve it. The best way is to embrace the goals and detailed plans.

It may take a while to determine your goals and plans but stick with it. Refer to your WHY statement continuously throughout the process. As we said before, you can write individual goal WHY statements if you find that this helps you. Be careful that the WHY statements align perfectly with your overall WHY statement. Enjoy the process of setting goals. Having discovered your WHY, you should have them on pieces of paper. It will be worth it in the end. Look at the bigger picture and the outcome to inspire you.

When you understand the clarity of your WHY statement, decision-making feels like a breeze. It will take you a little time to adjust to making decisions that support your real purpose in life, but after a short while, it becomes an automatic thing. Making the wrong decisions in life could cost—you'd do well to stay off that. The power of your WHY statement will remind you of the specific path you are on, and you will not dare decide on anything that will make you deviate from this path. For example, if the impact of your WHY statement relates to helping people achieve their goals, then don't do anything contrary. If a person requires your help to set their goals, you must be willing to offer yourself rather than allowing them to do it by themselves.

This is very important and closely related to the decisions that you make. As an extreme example, you cannot help others if you are drunk every evening or binge-watching Netflix. You need to make the right life choices that will enable you to live by your WHY statement. If your WHY statement is a far cry from the life you're living at the moment, then making a change will not be instantly. That's fine – you need to be persistent to get the best results. Stop being obsessed with money and focus on providing value to others. The money will come if you are truly committed to your WHY statement. It's not in any way going to be easy to live by your WHY statement--especially if your current lifestyle conflicts with it. Making a transition to a better life is never easy, as many people prefer to be pulled along in their lives. This is the least resistance they can put up. You are better than that. Now you need to turn this into your reality using all of the energy that you can muster. Create your WHY statement now!

THE MAGIC OF GRATITUDE

A re you on the path to finding your purpose but confused with no clear plan in sight? On the one hand, do you feel motivated to find your purpose but feel stuck with a go-with-the-flow type of life? Wherever you are standing in life, practicing gratitude has many benefits to help change your perspective and prime your mind to find your purpose. It can help accelerate the process. When you practice gratitude daily, you can achieve the following:

GRATITUDE CREATES VALUE IN YOUR LIFE AND CAREER

It's a no-brainer that you are more likely to succeed if you find meaning in your life and career. It doesn't matter what you do, simply being grateful that you are employed or healthy or having a home when so many others don't. During times of uncertainty, being grateful is a significant first step to finding your purpose. Gratitude could uncover the positives in the mundane and chaotic times in our lives. It can also help you stay focused passionately on the things you are grateful for. Being grateful for your job and your life creates a positive outlook to motivate you to stay on course until you excel.

GRATITUDE MAKES YOU A BETTER PERSON AND LEADER

When you're grateful for the people in your life, you'll interact better as you now see them from a different perspective, and that can make you a better person, friend, partner, or family member. In work, it will help you become a better coworker or manager. Practicing gratitude in your life will make you less critical, less overly demanding on all of your relationships, and less stressed. During chaos and uncertainty, living with less stress will create a more peaceful environment for your relationships. You then become more encouraging and supportive because you'll see the good in people. If you can trust and respect your team and your various relationships, it will ease tensions and create more loving, collaborative, and healthier relationships.

GRATITUDE PROMOTES PATIENCE & BETTER DECISION-MAKING

Grateful people are less likely to pursue instant gratification and are more patient. Being grateful for what you already have makes you less hasty in wanting more. This is a powerful mindset to have when it comes to making decisions in your life. When there's a lot of pressure in your life, a grateful mindset will see the bigger picture and make decisions based on long-term goals—instead of short-term satisfaction. Then your life is given meaning as you tap into your heart and your core.

GRATITUDE REDUCES STRESS IN LIFE & WORK

Gratitude helps cultivate patience, and patience cultivates acceptance. To this end, you'll be better prepared to handle the different changes in work and life, especially during times of uncertainty. We've all experienced chaotic and stressful days when the days seem so relentless with news after news, and it goes on and on. We know how draining and frustrating it could be when you feel like things are stressing you out, and things are springing out of control. With gratitude, you'll get the mental strength to work calmly, live more peacefully under pressure, and help avoid burnout and stress,-- which has a tremendous impact on your mental and physical well-being.

Gratitude is gaining the attention of so many people, especially in the field of positive psychology. When you practice it regularly, it has a significant impact on your well-being, health, and happiness. Gratitude improves your overall well-being. Various studies show that some of the emotional benefits of gratitude include content, peace, optimism, patience, and acceptance. Having these qualities allows you to be better prepared to handle life's challenges.

Gratitude also helps you sleep better. It promotes the relaxation response to the parasympathetic nervous system, ensuring a better ability to cope with stress and negative emotions. It also helps you exercise more, eat more, and be present to the benefits of having a healthy lifestyle. It helps strengthen your immune system and promotes faster healing and recovery. It reduces pain, lowers your blood pressure, gives you more energy, and lengthens your lifespan. Gratitude may have several benefits attached to it, but one of the most exciting is that it can mold your personality and transform your life. Research has shown that everyone loves being around a grateful person. They describe the person as being kind, humble, sympathetic, considerate, and supportive. You will experience positive change in your life when gratitude spills into everyone who comes in contact with you. As your circle grows, you'll be surrounded by like-minded people who appreciate you as much as you appreciate them.

HERE'S HOW YOU USE GRATITUDE TO FIND MEANING AND PURPOSE:

Adopt an Attitude of Gratitude and Create More Happiness

Most people seem to think it's going to come the other way around: I will be happy when I lose 5 pounds or when I get a promotion. I will become grateful when I'm involved in a loving relationship. Being grateful is a critical key to happiness because you appreciate what you already have. Anything else is extra, and that's great. When you're content with your life right now, that means you already know how to show appreciation when more comes - and it will. Practicing gratitude is not rocket science—it's as easy as a walk in the park. It costs nothing to get started, and it takes just a few minutes a day. Here are a few basic steps, along with some ways to integrate gratitude into your life.

START A GRATITUDE JOURNAL

Studies found that journaling is one of the best ways to keep gratitude in your mind daily. All you need to do is record three to five things you're grateful for in the morning and three things that you're grateful for in the evening, and what happened throughout the day. That way, you are conditioning your mind to find gratitude the first thing in the morning and the last thing before going to bed. I tend to do extra things like writing a couple more things in my gratitude journal; I write what I'm excited and committed to doing in the morning. For the past 5 years, I have made it a habit to keep a gratitude journal, and it has helped me tremendously and has changed my life. I would advise you to have a physical notebook or keep a digital notebook like Evernote.

BE MINDFUL OF OPPORTUNITIES FOR GRATITUDE

Here is another exercise if you want to adopt a gratitude lifestyle —especially when you're feeling overwhelmed and stressed. The first thing to do is close your eyes, take a deep breath throughout the day, reflect on the way you are, the sights and sounds, and the smells around you. Reflect on your surroundings and find what you're grateful for. This simple exercise will help you create a habit of gratitude, and you'll learn not to take anything for granted. Now let's do a bit of imaginative work. Imagine something happens at work, or you watch something on social media. If you felt stressed out and overwhelmed, shut it off immediately and then close your eyes for a minute, take a couple of deep breaths and start thinking about all the things you're grateful for in that exact moment. It could be as simple as being grateful for your heartbeat, being grateful for the glass of water in front of you, or being grateful that you can type with your fingers. Those may not make too much impact, but they carry enough power to turn your life around.

MORE TIPS ON LIVING A GRATITUDE LIFESTYLE

The importance of gratitude cannot be overemphasized. Make it a habit to give thanks before you eat your meal: whether you're religious or not, take a moment to pause before taking a bite of your food and say a short "thank you" that you're able to eat. It is also worth thanking the people who prepared the food, even if they're not physically present. Still, show gratitude if they happen to sit right in front of you. You can even share the meal with them. If you have a special person in your life, like someone that has helped you tremendously in the past, you could go out of your way to send voice messages and thank you cards. They could be your spouse, a friend, or your child.

When you show appreciation for things done in the past, it creates an atmosphere of love, and it fosters a greater relationship between you and the receiver. Take a walk: taking walks has greatly been underestimated to have benefits. Reflect on the fresh air, look at the trees, look at the ground, look at the cars around you, and look at the sky; it'll help you reflect on the environment we live in. Then look at the positives and the good that happens in the world and its environment. Focus on the little details and everything when you're taking a walk outside and allow yourself to be very content with the fact that you're taking a walk and enjoying being outside.

Thank salespeople and various service providers: Some people may just be having one of their bad days, especially if they're serving you. Selfishly and selflessly use gratitude to show in-depth appreciation to show how much you care. You can smile at them, a kind word, or say something that they did well. You can also compliment their attitude and service because it will motivate them to give more superior service and pass it on to other customers. Pour your gratitude to your children or your pets: whether you have children or pets, there's no doubt that you love them very much. Have you ever stopped to reflect on how much you love being around them, spend time loving them, giving them hugs and cuddles, or extra pampering? They will reflect that right back to you.

Offer to help someone: in showing appreciation to a colleague or a neighbor, you can offer to run an errand for them or do them a favor. The key is to be sincere, and you're offering to do it gracefully, knowing that you're going to help somebody out. People who are married or are in relationships tend to have more energetic and more positive relationships that allow your spouse and partner to see each other beyond your flaws and shortcomings. Grateful people enjoy doing mundane tasks and have a positive outlook that helps them find excitement and pleasure in things that they take for granted or find boring. Grateful people realize how precious life is and take nothing for granted.

These people express their gratitude consistently and have stronger family bonds and closer relationships. Also, they are never entitled to feel privileged and thankful for what they have achieved. They're humble and modest, which inspires respect, especially if they're highly successful. Grateful people are also liberated from materialism, overconsumption and the pursuit of material things because they're content with what they have and don't need instant gratification. They focus on relationships and experiences instead of material things that don't add value to their lives.

Imagine a life where everybody practices gratitude. Imagine what the world would look like if everyone engaged in such activity. At work, people would become more grateful and can have better relationships. Politicians would be less backstabbing, manipulative and tell fewer lies. The great news is that gratitude is extremely contagious, so start with yourself and become the change in your life and in your work for others to see; you'll be very impressed and amazed to see the results. Practicing gratitude and learning to appreciate things, people, and your environment despite what's happening in the world will change your life in different ways. In your life and work, it can open doors to advancement, new opportunities, and create a pleasant environment for you and others.

13

LEVERAGING MEDITATION

There are so many benefits to meditation—and countless number of them exist. Like gratitude, meditation is one of those practices that primes your mind and gets you in a space where you can find and deliver your purpose. According to a study published in JAMA Internal Medicine, mindful meditation can help reduce depression, anxiety, and pain. Dr. Elizabeth Hoge, a psychiatrist at Massachusetts General Hospital and an assistant professor of psychiatry at Harvard Medical School, says it makes perfect sense to treat anxiety with mindfulness meditation. "People with anxiety have a problem dealing with distracting thoughts that have too much power. They can't distinguish between a problem-solving thought and a nagging worry that has no benefit." In times of uncertainty, we all have a level of anxiety, and meditation can help with that.

One of the most compelling reasons to meditate is that the entire process itself is impressive. Meditation isn't dependent on a result but the fact that it is sublime, and it transports you into a state of tranquility, peace and awareness during the practice itself and not just at the end. The means do equal the end, and the training and practice of meditation have no beginning and never ends. Meditation is critical because we live in times of stress and uncertainty. Unwanted energies bombard us in the form of social media video clips, television noise pollution, arguments of people being angry with politics, and the world's injustice. We need to develop the superpower of controlling our mind and energy to counteract the overwhelming negativity and uncertainty in the world.

Meditation helps us connect to that internal space where we can cleanse our energy and develop a heightened sense of awareness of ourselves and our surroundings. When you start doing this, you can be better positioned to be in touch with your purpose. In the old days, people were surrounded by nature and their daily routines and rituals. There weren't things like telephones or technology. There wasn't any stress from any result of urban industrial complexities. There was a sound of the wind, water, beauty, stars that you could see clearly and the natural scent of the Earth.

There weren't the distractions that we have today. There were natural rhythms of different aspects of life as people planted seeds; they were in tune with the natural cycles of the Earth and felt connected to the land. We live our entire existence without connecting to nature; we live in artificial climates, keeping fruits that aren't natural and packaged in a factory. We only separate ourselves from anything natural. On top of that, various inequities exist on the Earth. We have a whole population of people that are entirely disconnected from nature and our internal power and energy.

Meditation serves as a bridge. It helps us with an easy and convenient way to enter a dimension in our lives that was utterly lost and divorced from natural rhythms. When we close the world around us and let go of our bodies and clear our minds of artificial stress, it consciously and unconsciously gets in tune with our lives. Again, it costs nothing, there are no side effects, and it won't add stress to your body like increased calories or high blood pressure. It's not addictive like drugs or alcohol, but you get a natural high when you do it the right way. The human brain is very complicated, and the body naturally produces drugs that are a hundred times more powerful than pharmaceuticals. When one meditates, the body secretes hormones and chemicals that provide a rush of energy and happiness, which is only one of the significant side effects of meditation.

Meditation is very different for everyone. Some people use it in place of psychotherapy. Others find it enhances their sports or work performance or increases mental functions like increasing your memory. Some people even use meditation to deal with grief or trauma or tragedy and increase appreciation for life in its beauties. Meditation also serves as a creative tool to help people with music and art and other creative fields. Meditation even helps us become more sustainable, increase sexual energy, remain calm, and help us get some sleep.

I've used meditation precisely to visualize my life purpose. At the start of my career, it was of immense benefits as I used it to visualize my tasks for the day and my goals. Whenever I go snowboarding, I'd find a comfortable place to practice meditation for 10-15 minutes—I'd sit down in the middle of the mountain, on the side of the run. The idea is to connect with nature. I'll look at the big mountain to visualize the "perfect" life and remain calm. Then I will derive an abundance of energy to keep me focused. I found myself taking more risks on and off the snowboard, and it gave me the confidence to pursue my goals. You need to understand that you can pursue your passions, harness and combine it with other things to uncover your purpose. Besides, there are many reasons to meditate and make the world a better and more peaceful place. Imagine when everyone finds their purpose, and peace is seen in our surroundings and everyone around us. It would reduce stress and help everyone to take a pause and dive deep into a mental oasis.

"Meditation is like a gym in which you develop the powerful mental muscles of calm and insight."
--Ajahn Brahm.

The scientist named Richard Davidson, Ph.D. (University of Badger State), has been considering long-term meditation and began studying in the 1970s. On the invitation of the 14th Dalai Lama, he studied the brains of Buddhist monks using technology. He began hooking them up to EEGs to record how they respond while meditating. He noticed that while meditating, they started to create new pathways in some regions of the mind. Through meditation, you can be the creator of your destiny. In your practice, you can focus on changing your life for the better. You'll have the ability to redefine yourself in any direction you desire. Your imagination only limits the power of visualization and being present. You release the unlimited potential of your mind when you meditate. The ability to change or alter your universe starts with a single thought in your mind.

Once humans harnessed fire, how could they forsee its effects on global warming? It's just one of the many thousands of examples of the power of the mind; it's like cause and effect. The more you're in tune with what's going on in your mind and how you visualize it, it may seem small, of course, but it'll have a ripple effect throughout the world. A lot of change can happen in your purpose, but you can redefine it first in your mind. I remember the date like it was yesterday when I just realized that I should be starting my nonprofit. It was because I was completely in the moment; I closed my eyes and took deep breaths. I looked at the mountains, listened to the wind in the trees, with no leaves rustling. Then everything became utterly still, and that's when the seed of my nonprofit came to my mind.

Again, meditation is just a small part of the key to cultivating your purpose. I'm excited to share some of my meditation tips and how I used it to find my purpose. Among the documented benefits of meditation are: less anxiety, decreased depression, reduced irritability and moodiness, better learning ability and memory, and greater creativity. That's just for starters. Then there are slower aging (possibly due to higher DHEA levels), feelings of vitality and rejuvenation, less stress (actual lowering of cortisol and lactate levels), rest (lower metabolic and heart rate), lower blood pressure, and higher blood oxygen levels.

A SIMPLE MEDITATION TECHNIQUE

Most first-time meditators find it difficult to sit in silence, sit down with their innermost thoughts and emotions, sit down without doing a thing — those very things that the mind wants to avoid. Meditation might initially feel a little alien to a beginner, maybe even daunting, but that's fine. People have been meditating for around 3,000 years, and many have certainly endured the same trepidation, reticence, or wonder that is often felt by first-time meditators. Here's a simple technique to lead into the process of meditation and give you results in minutes: Sit comfortably, close your eyes, and tense up your whole body. Sigh deeply, then breathe deeply through your nose and release the tension from every muscle. Just feel each part relaxing, watching for parts that may hold onto tension, like a tight jaw.

If you still have tension somewhere, tense up that part again, then let it relax. It may also help to repeat silently "relax" as the tension drains. This will train your body and mind to recognize relaxation. Later, you may be able to relax more quickly just by repeating "relax" a few times. Breathe through your nose. This is important because it brings in more oxygen by involving your diaphragm more. You can test this. Breathe with your mouth, and you'll notice that your breathing is shallower. Then breathe through your nose, and you'll notice that your abdomen extends more. Air is being drawn deeper into your lungs.

Allow your breathing to fall into a comfortable pattern and

pay attention to it. Pay attention to your breath as it passes in and out of your nose. Your mind may wander endlessly, but all you have to do is continually bring attention back to your breath. If your mind is still too busy, try identifying the distractions to set them aside. For example, say in your mind, "itchy leg," "worried about work," or "anger," and then immediately return attention to your breathing. Use any means you can to identify and set aside distractions. That's it. Continue for five or ten minutes, or 100 breaths. Afterward, open your eyes and sit there for a few seconds. You'll feel relaxed, and your mind will feel refreshed. And you'll be better prepared for any mental challenges. That's how to meditate.

Well, that technique may seem too challenging for you—but relax, I still got you covered. One of the best things I do is to open up youtube.com and search for "10 minutes guided meditation" or "20 minutes guided meditation." That was how I stumbled on the work of Dr. Joe Dispenza, and he's got a fantastic 25-minute evening meditation that you can engage in before bed and 25-minute morning meditation. Embrace it and practice it. There are many resources available on meditation. Those new to the practice may opt to take part in a class or guide at the beginning. Others may prefer to read up on the various options and practice —on their own. Go online to search for books and resources or visit a yoga or spiritual center. Meditation can be an enjoyable experience and provide balance to an otherwise hectic life.

14

CREATING UNYIELDING PASSION

One way you can find your purpose is by aggressively pursuing your passions. We spent a good chunk of the book talking about passion, and it cannot be underestimated. Who knows, you may be able to make a living from it. Although that's not the goal, it's about finding what lights you up and then using that fuel to serve yourself and impact others' lives through your purpose. If you're feeling stuck in your current life and confused about where to begin, taking that bold step to find your path and taking action will lead you to your purpose.

One way to start looking at ways to explore your passions is to figure out your comfort zones. Are you in a place where you feel very comfortable? Well, that's not a good place for you to grow and find your purpose. So if you've been doing the same routines without excitement, perhaps you need to look into other areas to find what lights you up. Are you living the life that you truly want? If not, then start thinking of possible risks you can take to achieve that lofty goal.

When I took the giant leap to pursue my nonprofit organization, I started looking at other areas out of my comfort zone. One of the things that came to mind was taking an acting class. I was not sure if I wanted it, but I embraced it because the desire to get out there and do something new was so strong. It turned out to be of great benefit—I became more comfortable in large gatherings. At some point, I was a leader of a group and could air my voice. One of the ways to finding your purpose is looking beyond your comfort zone and seeking new things.

I know that following your passion brings a sense of power and awakens you to the beauty that resides in the outside world. Passion comes from the heart; it's almost like a spiritual journey, and it changes your thoughts, perceptions and feelings. Finding your passion and aggressively pursuing it can be daunting, but it also can lead to a vibrant life that opens you up to hopes, wishes, and dreams.

PURSUING THE PURPOSE

Speak your truth clearly: To find your passion, you have to speak your truth and be prepared for new adventures. You should know what matters to you, the things that make you happy, complete and authentic. You might also want to know what you're good at.

Be open for support: You're not isolated and need support from the right friends, family, and positive social circle to help you reach your goals.

Open up your senses: If you follow the paths of gratitude and meditation, you will open up your thoughts to understand what lights you up, like things that give you peace, serenity, even motivation, and make your heart warm. That's what you should go after. You'll be more patient to find what you're passionate about. Then you'll realize the in and out of your control.

Give yourself time for pleasure: You should be easy on yourself, be kind and grateful as much as possible—not too hard because you're pursuing your passion to uncover your purpose. You have to allow yourself to go for the things that give you pleasure. You may feel self-centered and guilty because you're not productive and potentially serving others, but there will be time for that in the future. This actual view of pleasure is about getting to know yourself and helping you get to the root of the essentials that matter in your life. It is an exploration about you. These gentle pleasures are good for your health, and they're very productive; ultimately, you'll become more focused and find your passion.

Liberate yourself: Someone who finds their passion is, in some ways, a wise person. Taking time to do this reflects your personality and values, leading to a lifelong pursuit of happiness and contentment. You'll feel a sense of lightness when you accept who you are—you don't need others' approval to do this. When you accept who you are, people will start to accept who you are as well. The human mindset is holistic, and part of knowing it will put to rest the constant struggle of trying to seek the acceptance of others.

Strengthen yourself through affirmations: Affirmations are critical if you want to make headway in life. It enables you to be more optimistic and secure about reaching your goals. People who are lost don't reach their destination because of fear of failure. When you allow yourself to go through the ups and downs, it reminds you to get back up when you fail.

The world news may not help or even your friends. Their perception is that everything going on is negative, and that makes it impossible for you to pursue your purpose and achieve it. In times of chaos and uncertainty, beautiful creations rear their heads, and this is an opportunity to pursue your passion. It's not easy to shut these people out, but by creating a sense of affirmations for yourself, it's almost like the daily mantra that gives you the energy to wade off negative energies that try to come into your life and shut you down. Some people spend their whole life looking for what they want to do or where they want to take their journeys. I'm going to help you do this in a fast and efficient way. You'll be presented with the essentials when it comes to finding your passion in life--and it's never too late to find it.

If my mother of almost 80 years could still discover her passions, you can do the same. It's not an easy feat having a firm grasp over your calling; you might have to go through different roads to find it. So here are some tips that you can follow:

Look at things around you: Determine what and who inspires you to achieve your set goals. Are there people out there who have the life you wish or have accomplished things that you set out for yourself? What are the objects that create some spark and enhance you to move forward? Use these objects and the people to narrow down your passions. Listing them down will help you navigate your way with ease.

Have happy thoughts: Go back into your past and reminisce about what made you happy in your youth. It would help if you also thought of the last time you experienced that exciting moment. If it was already a long time ago, what do you think caused that state?

What ignited your passion in the past? Reading your favorite book? Watching your favorite movie or documentary? If you can't find what ignited your passion in the past, start drawing inspiration on little things that did.

You're stuck in a job for the money: It's going to be hard to find your real passion if you continue in that job cringe every morning you jump off the bed. You probably never liked the job, but you took it up anyway. What were you thinking at that point? What were your career choices before now? Who did you want to be when you graduated from college or when you were growing up? One of the things that you should consider doing is saving up enough money or finding a way to stash money to quit your current job. By doing this, you'll be able to buy a lot of time to pursue that thing before it's too late.

You have to be open to new possibilities: You'll need to expect more than what you already have if you want to acquire and reach any real level beyond your comfort zone. Expect higher for yourself and expect higher from situations and relationships. Again, taking risks is going to help you; it doesn't matter where you are as long as you get started and that you start going towards the things that truly excite you.

Finding your passion is an endless song. When you do the things that you are passionate about, you let your life flourish. You let yourself connect to everything you are in mind, heart, and spirit. You are stronger and can face challenges better because you are reinforced by doing the things you love. You feel more alive, positive, self-respecting, and determined. You live your life with confidence and high morale. And you feel you are contributing goodness and positivism to the people in your life.

15

VOLUNTEERING FOR IMPACT

The demands placed on our daily lives can easily become overwhelming. We are busy, overwhelmed, and stressed, and there is never enough time for us. Why should we engage in volunteer work? How would we devote ourselves to helping others if it takes more of our time and makes us feel stressed? The reality is that volunteering will change your life just as much as those you're supporting. You become a member of a larger community when you volunteer. You network with unique and incredible people, and you have the opportunity to learn about new sectors and fields.

When you donate your current skills, you'll be able to improve them more and gather some more as you make progress. Volunteering service can also give rise to new career opportunities. Have you ever wanted to work for a nonprofit? Do you have a special interest in the service industry? Volunteering can be a perfect way to get your foot in the door, and once you get there, you may not even know you want it until you get onboard. Volunteering moved me closer to finding my purpose. I enjoyed serving others, and it felt like I was having fun while at it. I wanted to impact lives, and the perfect avenue was through nonprofit work.

"The most selfish thing to do is to serve others."
    -Marie Larosiliere

Here's why that quote makes sense. When you give yourself to others and serve them, you receive so much more in return—sometimes, even more than the people you're helping. So, whenever I give to others, I give to myself. This concept has been ingrained in my head, and I always want to give my all. I believe that every positive thing I do benefits the people I'm helping and myself. We all receive what we give to others. So when I started this journey of finding purpose, I decided that I was going to serve others and continue serving because it will lead me to discover myself. I will learn to be a leader and the person I envisioned in the future.

I enjoy doing things for others. I know that it impacts my life, and it allows me to feel excellent about myself. I get a lot of self-confidence when I'm kind to others, and the good acts of kindness always come back to me—many times more. I'm generous to a fault with my time, attention, and money. One of the things that I avoid is making my life complicated with acts of generosity. So when I do it, it's very straightforward. I serve others when my life is stable, and I'm in control. I also embark on this selfless service when I feel I'm in a place to serve.

Here are some critical questions to ask before serving others:

- When have I benefited by helping others first?
- How do I feel when I make life better for others?
- In what positive ways could my life change if I did more for others?

Here's one of the biggest secrets to getting what you want

and finding your purpose: picking a cause and going all in from a volunteer and philanthropic perspective. There are so many different benefits from it, but people often wait until they become successful or find their purpose. If you are proactive, giving back can lead you to your purpose. So, if you've ever wanted to become a philanthropist or charitable, why wait when you can do something right now?

In times of uncertainty, there is usually a community that needs your help and support. Participating in cause-minded work will be one way to find your purpose and become more peaceful and balanced. Then you'll gain perspective. You don't need a million-dollar foundation to start a nonprofit. You don't need huge funds to make that bold statement. What you need is your commitment to serve. Many causes need your help: social injustice to education, the environment, children's diseases, and hospitals. It's about approaching a particular cause and contributing your part to lessen the community's problems. Think of the injustices in the world, especially the ones that frustrate you. Is social injustice, police brutality, or institutional racism something that triggers you?

Here is more information about finding organizations that provide solutions in that regard. Go to guidestar.org or ask your friends for recommendations regarding nonprofits doing great work in the field. This will give you a perspective on how effective they have been. You can do the same thing with any because that triggers you. One of the first things I usually do is narrow down my list to two or three organizations, then donate to them. I stay on their mailing list, follow them on social media, find out what they're doing and get involved. Suppose they have meetings, volunteer opportunities, or means to advance the cause using a well-defined support strategy. Then I would actively get involved and try to connect with their supporters. If they have events or meetings, I will show up and listen to them first before asking questions to get clarity on how to contribute. You can go the same route if you're passionate about contributing to the cause.

Another approach to becoming more philanthropic and charitable is giving a thought to how you ended up here in life. Are you a child of a single parent? Are you a child of immigrants? Was education critical to you and your family, and did that help you become successful? Did you go to summer camp? Are you a survivor of abuse or the foster care system? Are there specific causes that you can search for? I was a child of immigrant parents who had foster children. I also always wanted to snowboard growing up, and I loved to skateboard. I didn't realize that this was a set up for things to come. My mentorship program took center stage with kids, helping them make better career choices alongside their school work. They also learned how to acquire life skills. The gap in the mentoring field led me to start my nonprofit organization.

Think back to what happened in your life and figure out what led to you being where you are today. There's usually a cause that is solving the same problem. And then again, you would do what I've mentioned above to see how you can get involved with a cause personal to you. There is a simple thing you need to do, which is not even about going to a nonprofit. You need to start a little initiative on your own. Are there homeless people in your community? Is there a school in your community? During wintertime, you can create different care packages with food, snacks, socks, hand warmers, toothbrushes, toothpaste, and toiletry kits for the homeless. Put these packages together, and as you're driving, distribute them to homeless people you see on the street. Those are little things you can do to make a difference.

If there's a school, email the principal to figure out how you can get involved. Go to their website to dig out their email address.

Your email should read:

Dear (name of principal)
I live in the community, and I wondered if
there are volunteer opportunities, or if
you need help to improve the school. I
would love to have a meeting with
you. I'm looking forward to hearing
back from you.

Best Regards,
Your Name

Often, they have a PTA or someone on their staff to point you in the right direction. Maybe they need a cleanup. Maybe they need a career day speaker. It could also be a basketball or soccer coach, a classroom painted, or school supplies for their incoming class. You can then organize your fundraiser on gofundme.com, telling people what you're doing and how it can change lives. Raise money and deliver it on your own. You can do this without starting a nonprofit organization. It will help you develop a sense of purpose in helping people and navigating institutions in different communities. Lastly, volunteering can help your personal and career growth tremendously.

I have years of experience running a nonprofit and seeing lives changed by people's involvement in a cause, so here are five ways people can grow personally and professionally by volunteering with a nonprofit:

EVERYBODY WINS

The agency or organization you work for gets some tasks completed without paying someone to do them. When you find yourself in a nonprofit, you're fulfilled doing what you love while the organization meets the needs of so many people in the community. It's a win-win.

YOU'LL EXPAND YOUR HORIZONS

If you're a social butterfly, you'll make new friends. If you're quiet and shy, volunteering will facilitate your skills. It's not unusual for volunteers to discover they share common likes and interests with staff members. You'll be exposed to entirely new environments, depending on where you choose to help out. You'll meet new people and experience new things.

REDEFINING PROFESSIONAL IMAGE

You'll learn new skills that will help you in both your personal and professional life. Often, organizations that utilize volunteers don't require you to have specific skills at first. Therefore, you "hit the ground running." This can be incredibly exciting and enriching because you'll have opportunities to discover new abilities and practice new skills. Also, there's a real possibility that you'll expand your business network. Coming into contact with a diverse group of people may provide possible job opportunities.

REFRESH YOUR JOB-HUNTING EFFORTS

Giving your time and energy into a volunteer project allows you to escape from your routine. When you volunteer, you'll become invigorated with new energy, passion, and drive. You'll be reminded of the skills you have, the confidence you hold, and the energy you expend when you're doing a job.

A GREAT FEELING ABOUT HELPING OTHERS

Giving to others can evoke beautiful feelings within you and the people you help. Knowing that you've made a real contribution to a community will enrich your life in countless ways. Helping people in need brings out your true humanity. You'll be reminded that everyone needs assistance at some point in life, and you'll be humbled by the experience when you meet needs that matters. Deciding to volunteer first involves taking a look at your current situation so that you can fit this activity into your schedule regularly. Investigate your volunteer possibilities and go for it! Embrace all of the enriching experiences that come with volunteering. When you give back, you'll experience things in the real world and see how others live. Giving back to the community brings fulfillment. Volunteering is the first step!

16

BUILDING NETWORKS & COMMUNITY

B uilding networks and a community around yourself is one of the most important things you could do to find your purpose. When you tap into value-oriented relationships, you open up opportunities to share ideas, get potential collaborators, and then form experiences from the people that you know. If you're not actively building your networks, you're missing out on a fantastic opportunity to grow personally, professionally, and find your purpose. Here are the benefits of building networks and building a community around yourself:

INCREASED OPPORTUNITIES

When you build your networks, you open up to more opportunities that you wouldn't otherwise have. Whether it is partnerships, personal relationships, love, mentorship, or speaking engagements, you'll be more open to taking them up when joining different networks.

INCREASED BUSINESS

One of the main benefits of building a network is getting more business deals. When you are in a community of people with similar interests, your goal would be to serve them personally and professionally, ultimately leading to finding your purpose.

CONTACTS / RELATIONS

You've heard the expression that "it is not what you know; it's who you know." When you build connections, you open your life and business to different resources. You'll meet new people who share your beliefs and values.

ADVISORS / MENTORS

When you network, you could be meeting people who have a wealth of knowledge and resources. You can learn so much from your network if you take advantage of it. You may even meet people who understand your goals and can connect you to your purpose. They may be excited to help you realize it. That way, you'll bypass months of trial and error learning to do it yourself.

BECOMING KNOWN

You will become known if you repeatedly show up in a community network, contributing and sharing value with the group. Again, you will gain some notoriety in a particular field or industry or type of community. For example, if you're into entrepreneurship, and your part of an entrepreneur community, you always show up to support and help many people. That will let people know you for what you do. Imagine if you do that in any other field? Opportunities can spring up, and your purpose can manifest through what you add to the community.

STAYING POSITIVE

You need to surround yourself with positive people and those of like-minds, who support you and your goals. It will naturally rub off on you and help you thrive as a person and give you a sense of purpose.

IT'S A CONFIDENCE BUILDER

Building networks and joining the community will impact your self-confidence. You'll be so surprised at how you become more comfortable around people if you aren't. The more you get involved in this cause, the better you get at it, so you don't give up.

YOU MAKE NEW FRIENDS

One of the best parts is making new friends through the community. Often, there are people you didn't grow up with or went to school with, but you share something in common. You can gain a lot of knowledge and insight by having a good friend based on your community's shared interest.

Here's what to do when networking. Building your networks and communities is very potent, and you want to make sure that you do it right; otherwise, you can mess up your confidence. With low confidence, throwing in the towel becomes a constant thought. On the contrary, you need a community to fulfill your purpose.

KNOW YOUR INTENDED OUTCOME

The idea is to find your purpose and meet people who have found theirs. Such environments encourage you to pursue your purpose vigorously. The support you get from people who have been on this journey before now is vital.

BE SMART ABOUT ANSWERING QUESTIONS

You must learn how to answer common questions—and answer them in a way that invites more questions and further connects you with people. The typical type is "what do you do?" When you're networking, don't tell people what you do; instead, tell them what you'll be doing in the future. I remember when I started, I kept telling people about my nonprofit. I told them what I was working on for my nonprofit. At any given moment, I could have told them what I did in the past or the present. However, I focused on telling them what I was planning to do.

Here is a piece of advice if you're asked the question, "What do you do?"—if you're struggling to find your purpose or at a crossroads regarding what to do, it would be best to say you're seeking to make a meaningful impact in the world, and right now, you're exploring. Most people will like your response and offer to help. You could feel bad when they come at you that way because they appear to know what they're doing. Listen, you don't have to. If some people have it all figured out, inquire about them and ask how they found their purpose. When you're looking for purpose, you are looking for brief sparks of inspiration, and by networking and building communities, you're tapping into the experience of others to find yours.

MAKE A GOOD FIRST IMPRESSION

The next thing is to make a good first impression. Smile at people and then give a good handshake. Speak less of yourself and make others feel important—it's critical when networking. So you can ask where people are from and what their interests are. What breaks the ice for me is asking what Netflix shows they're watching. This strategy helps me connect with people on a human level. When you meet people face-to-face, find points of connection, ask them what they need help with and what challenges they're facing in their business. Know as much about them, especially if you want to keep them in your contact list. You could ask what books they are reading and why they read them. You could even draw some inspiration from what they have learned from the books. That's how I keep in contact with people. I also read a lot of books, so I recommend certain books to people. I've bought books for people if I thought they would get value from them. That simple gesture helps me have better connections. I connect with them on LinkedIn, Facebook, and Instagram. I also engage with their content if it's somebody I'd like to develop a better relationship with. If you want to zero in on building a community that works, you will set goals to meet certain people every week. By keeping track of them, you benefit in the long run.

EXPRESS GRATITUDE

Express gratitude to them. If you notice that the person, you're engaging in a conversation with is thoughtful or detail-oriented, be intentional and say, "You know what I've noticed, you are (insert nice quality here). I find that to be a very admirable quality; you must be very good at your job." This approach helps you connect better with people. If you want to take things to the next level with the relationship, express a certain vulnerability level. When you go this route, you're trying to break the barriers to enable you to accelerate the relationship.

DELIVER ON YOUR PROMISES

If you promise something, deliver on it. If someone promises, follow up, but don't be too pushy. When they refuse to follow through on their promise, note that and move on. They may not be the type of person you want to develop a quick relationship with. If they're worth it, then give them more time.

The Don'ts of Networking

DON'T SELL ANYTHING

Don't forward anything political or religious unless the group is around politics or religion or anything that is a potentially sensitive topic. Also, don't talk too much about yourself; you should be finding out more about other people and making them feel important.

DON'T TALK ABOUT YOUR CHALLENGES OR PERSONAL FLAWS

Regardless of the challenges you're facing or flaws, don't say it out. Only do so when you overcome them.

DON'T BE AFRAID TO ASK QUESTIONS

Everybody is afraid to appear stupid or dumb, but there is no need. The overwhelming majority of people will love to increase their knowledge and expertise, so make sure you ask as many questions as possible.

STOP OVERZEALOUS SELF-PROMOTION

This tactic would be more irritating than creating meaningful relationships.

DON'T GET DRUNK

This is very important, especially at more informal meet-ups, where they could be serving alcohol. Becoming intoxicated is the worst thing you might do when networking or building community.

So you may be wondering how you go out there and network with people. It is not as hard as you think. Just go out and meet people—it's as simple as that.

LOOK TO YOUR COMMUNITY

You can go into your local community; some events happen at coffee shops or even the Chamber of Commerce if you're in business. You can also go to sites like Eventbrite, Craigslist, Facebook to see what events are based on your interests and passion. Even places like social clubs, gyms, and yoga studios have different events that you can attend. So, I would use any of all those opportunities to network and build community.

ATTEND FUNDRAISING EVENTS

Attend fundraisers to get more involved with nonprofits and volunteering. I love using this strategy to build networks because you are building community around a common cause. It also shows you are a supportive person, and you can get behind supporting a community in need. The types of people that attend fundraisers are usually people you want to be around. Even if it's a charity golf tournament, gala or a bowling event, it is a great way to meet people who share similar interests and causes with you, and you can find your purpose through such mediums.

USE PEOPLE YOU KNOW

A great way to network is to use the people that you know. Remember, people that you have in your network may be the ones to help you find your purpose. Leverage your network by putting out an offer to help someone. If you have a graphic design skill, you can put out an offer to have the job delivered at a reduced price or create free donation-based design work for people with small business ideas. Better still, you can go to your current network and say, "Hey, I'm looking to meet someone in entertainment or filmmaking," or "I'm looking to meet someone with experience in real estate." Then you can get recommendations within your network. The important thing is to ensure that you maintain all of your relationships and not lose track of them. You can do this online by creating different lists on Facebook or Twitter.

Remember to re-evaluate your network and your needs, and perhaps the needs of the people you have in your network. However, if you find that someone is too needy, it might be worthwhile to cut them loose. Don't burn bridges in the process, but be mindful of people's needs and what you're capable of giving to them. So, I leverage this strategy to build up my network and strengthen my purpose personally.

Before starting my nonprofit, I had built a network of nonprofit professionals. One of the ways that I strengthened and developed a better community was by hosting events. I hosted an event every first Friday of every month, and the venue was at a bar. I was the DJ and one of the hosts. I would get other nonprofit professionals from different organizations to co-host with me. So everybody would have to invite 5 to 10 people each. The music and drinks would come from my end; it was a great way to build community amongst young nonprofit professionals. 10% of the bar sales would go to me, so it was a nice little bonus.

The essence of the event was to learn about different nonprofits and get great ideas from them. These professionals created a pathway to launch my first nonprofit. I was able to find a non-profit partner through that network and developed lots of relationships. I would also recruit volunteers for my organizations through just that simple strategy. The interesting thing is, I was able to move out of my comfort zone. Being introverted, I defied the odds and hosted an event. I was surprised at myself (but that's what happens when you seek purpose). I became more of a leader and a public speaker.

17

HACKING SOCIAL CHALLENGES

S ocial challenges have been very popular as of late and are ways for businesses to gain new customers and followers for their social and web platforms. As a participant, there are great ways to learn about something new, develop yourself, or get an idea off the ground in community with other people. The power of community and momentum to do things as a group and seeing the collective results makes it a powerful medium for people to tie together their personal or professional goals in a time-sensitive manner. When you go the community route, you build trust, and you build new relationships to become more productive. The potential for exponential growth is enormous when you're doing and learning new things at the same time. If you're looking to find your purpose and learn skills along the way, a social challenge may be your best bet.

So, it might sound weird as to why a social challenge might help you find your purpose. One of the main reasons to take part is that it's an easy way to learn new things about yourself and connect to people that you may not ordinarily meet to uncover your passion and then find your purpose. For instance, there are a lot of Instagram influencers who host Instagram challenges, and that could be the perfect way to connect with them. You may have been struggling to master Instagram marketing for your business or even create valuable content for your niche market. With interest in growing your brand and self-expressing yourself creatively on Instagram, that could be a great jump start for you, and it could lead to other things in the future related to your purpose. These influencers have small groups online that you can be a part of. Every day, you'll get a set of tasks, and it is a fun and easy way to follow through a path to achieve an intended goal.

So how do you benefit? I use them to accomplish a set of tasks. I jumped on one challenge called #75hard. It was created by Andy Frisella, the CEO of 1st Phorm—a supplement company. For 75 days, you're supposed to exercise for 45 minutes twice a day. One of the exercises must be outdoors. You have to stick to a diet, read ten pages of a personal development or business book, then take a progress picture. And lastly, you round it off by drinking a gallon of water. If you miss anything throughout the day, you'll have to start over from day one. You can learn more at 75hard.com and follow hashtag #75hard. I lost 15 pounds. It took me four attempts to achieve that goal. Many people may consider it a fitness challenge, but it was more of a mindset challenge. Some of the things I learned were to commit to something and stick to it. It opened me up to facing challenges and don't give up until I win. I learned how much time is wasted during the day and how important it is to seize every moment when to a challenge.

This is one of the challenges that changed my life and helped me commit to writing this book. Putting pen to paper to flesh out my life isn't an easy process. I motivated myself to deliver on this project, working with a deadline to get me up and doing. Regardless of what may come through, I was determined to finish it. Social challenges propelled me to move forward to achieve other things. I joined another challenge, this time on how to build a Facebook group. Riding on the success of the last challenge, I created my Facebook group within one week called the "Hustlers of Good."

You may have deduced from the two challenges that the chances of success are higher once you set a goal with a deadline in mind and have other people working on the same thing as you. One of the things to consider is where you are mentally and time-wise. Do you have the time to participate in a challenge? Think about your goals or a list of things you've always wanted to achieve. It often boils down to finding the right influencer or thought leader who is very active and engaged with their community. Then find a set of skills you'd like to learn, whether it's social media management or photography—or even writing. There are different ways that you can participate; search on social media.

Right now, I create challenges for myself, and I do them within 30 days without fail. I keep track of my progress by creating spreadsheets to get in tune with my daily routine, and I also build accountability around my goals, so I can talk about them with people. What I love about "challenges" is that they are specific: what do you want to accomplish? Why do you want to achieve it, and what are you looking to take away from it? They're also time-based and come with a deadline. They're relevant to my goals and my passions. I can measure them as I can see progress daily. I wish you could imbibe this concept and run with it to find your purpose.

18

WHY YOU NEED A SIDE HUSTLE

This is one of the strategies I've used to find my purpose and build skills and create opportunities. When I was starting my nonprofit, I viewed it as a side project or a project. I coined it as a "project mindset" technique. When you have a project mindset, you're launching a series of experiments in the form of a project or a side business that will hopefully lead to finding your purpose. I had no skill to kick-start my nonprofit organization, but I knew I wanted it badly. So, I viewed it as a way to get an idea off the ground. Being passionate about mentoring and snowboarding kept me on the right track, but I needed to merge the two passions. The idea was to do a snowboard mentoring project and then use that experience and my marketing background to apply to the University of British Columbia for a Master's in Business Administration. That was the big idea that I came up with while I was snowboarding in British Columbia, and I fell in love with that part of Canada. I had no idea that the project would take off so well, and it would end up being a 15-year career. It was the missing link to finding my purpose in life.

The first thing you want to do is start listing out all your different hopes, wishes, dreams, and how they can be somewhat applied to a project. The project is usually something that serves a community or a need. I created one-sheet, and I listed "the why," "the how", "the when," and "the who." I started asking critical questions about how I could flush out the idea even more, and the next thing I knew was one sheet ended up being two to three pages. I thought about what skills I need to know and who I need to meet to get this idea off the ground. Then I went ahead and started building it. Through word of mouth, I started to get the word out. I kept motivating myself, and my goal was tied around accountability; I also wanted to keep my promise and get the ideas off the ground. With so much energy put out there, the organization took off, and we've been able to impact the lives of 10,000 people over 15 years.

There were other projects that aligned with my purpose while building skills and community along the way. A couple of years ago, I started an Instagram account for skateboarders. It was different; it was a motivational skateboarding Instagram account. I put motivational quotes over videos of skateboarding tricks. At one point, that account got up to 50,000 followers, and it gave me the opportunity to start creating new brands online. I incidentally developed a passion for Instagram. It also connected me with the core skateboard community, and that eventually benefited my nonprofit organization. You'll realize that once you find your purpose, you'll start coming up with new ways to create pathways and projects to enhance your purpose.

Now, let me tell you a little about my latest project. It was a business I started in the lumber and sawmill industry, which was out of my realm, but still served my purpose. My experience with Instagram came through. I started my account and created a hashtag to build a community around that idea. I've also created a podcast to add a voice and connect me with different professionals in the lumber and sawmill industry. I was flown all over the United States, even Europe, to speak about the lumber and sawmill industry. It all started because of my passion for entre-preneurship and business, and I got the spark and inspiration from my father-in-law, who had his own sawmill business. I wanted to help these small business owners gain the skills and the networks to grow a successful business based on their passion for the wood industry. It all led to my purpose, and the reason is simple—I love showing people the path to succeed so that they can live happy, healthy, and successful lives doing something they love.

This is something that I've done myself, so now I'm helping others do the same. That business has gone on to do exception-ally well. I've learned a lot of new skills and tapped into a whole new network of people and built a completely different commu-nity than I usually know. There are so many ways to create a project or a side hustle. You can start a blog or a photography Instagram account. You can create a podcast. Anything creative that gets your ideas and thoughts fleshed out will be perfect. If you want, you can create a different 6-week project, something you can work on for a short time of 6 weeks, then move on to the next if you have multiple ideas. It is a great way to balance out what's going on in your life with something creative. The best way to go ahead and do this is by getting inspiration from YouTube and other ideas and businesses that you may have stumbled on online. Lastly, be diligent about learning new skills. For me, I learned and became an expert at online marketing, lead generation, and social media advertising.

19

FORMING A MASTERMIND

You can ask any successful person, and they will tell you they didn't achieve success alone. It is no secret that many top entertainers, athletes, and business people had top-notch mentors who paved the way for them. There are moments when businessmen, women and entrepreneurs are left in a confused state. They feel helpless, lost, without any chance to survive, and then throw in the proverbial towel. For people who know better, however, masterminds provide solace and relief. Masterminds are a haven for people looking to develop their expertise and learn, while networking with some of the most innovative marketing and business minds in the world at the same time. Napoleon Hill found that the main reason why many entrepreneurs are highly successful and others are not is because the successful ones were part of a mastermind.

I didn't discover the power of masterminds until much later when I was developing my purpose. I first learned about masterminds from Napoleon Hill and his book *"Think and Grow Rich."* In chapter 10, Napoleon talks about mastermind as a "Coordination of knowledge and effort, in a spirit of harmony, between two or more people, for the attainment of a definite purpose." This theory is that no individual does one thing by themselves without the power and being in partnership with other people. Usually, there are two reasons people would form a mastermind, one for business, and the other is for mindset. So, what exactly is the goal of my group? It's a place to teach, learn, give, and receive support, and even brainstorm. It's usually a member of a group who provides accountability to each other; they often meet weekly or have monthly meetings. For my nonprofit, I have done things on my own. With the experience that I have garnered over the years, I would form a mastermind if I were to start a business now. A mastermind can consist of people with shared interests and shared desires; it could be business owners, creative people, or people working towards being on the same path, like finding purpose.

Why Create a Mastermind Group?

NEW IDEAS

Two heads are better than one. Ten heads can be even better. If you need help finding a solution to a challenge, a mastermind group can be of great help. You can also learn from each other. Everyone in the group has something to teach the other members.

SUPPORT

Do you need emotional support or encouragement? Do you need an expert to help you with something? A mastermind group can provide that too.

ACCESS TO NEW PARTNERS

Maybe you need a business partner or a loan. Perhaps you're looking for playdates or help with homeschooling of your child. Mastermind groups often have members that are looking for opportunities.

SOCIAL CIRCLE OF LIKE-MINDED PEOPLE

Many of your mastermind group members are like you. There are shared interests and similarities. You can add significantly to your social circle by joining or starting a group.

A NEW LEVEL OF THINKING

A mastermind group can expose you to others that have achieved much more than you. If you don't, then your goals suffer. Your lofty goals suddenly go conservative, and that may propel you to start thinking in a different way. You'll strive for higher levels of success when your part of a mastermind group.

ACCOUNTABILITY

Everyone in the group knows what you're working on. They'll hold you to your plans. There are many mastermind groups already. You might be able to find one online. Take a look around and see if there's a group that meets your needs. If you can't find a group, you can start one. I have certainly created one with people from four different states, and we met every Wednesday at 5 am Central for a year and a half, and it fast-tracked my development as an entrepreneur.

TIPS TO CREATING A MASTERMIND GROUP

Decide on the topic and purpose: When you advertise or contact prospective members, you need to be clear on what type of person you're looking for. Is your mastermind group for internet marketers or stay-at-home dads? What are you hoping to accomplish with the group? They should have something to offer and should receive benefits from being part of the group. Be picky. Your mastermind doesn't have to be too big. Focus on quality over quantity. Seek to build a high-quality group with high-quality members.

Look for people with different skills. The members should be similar but not exactly the same. For example, your group might be focused on real estate investing. It would be nice to have a builder, a banker, and a broker in it. Members should have similar levels of commitment. Ensure that everyone has the same level of drive as you do. A group with both serious and casual members will be dysfunctional. There are even paid mastermind groups to make sure there are serious levels of commitment.

Determine the frequency and format of meetings. How often will you meet? How will the meetings be conducted? Will one person run the meeting? Will it be the same person each time? All the members will have to decide these details. Expect everyone to contribute. People shouldn't be allowed just to gain a benefit from the meetings. They should be expected to provide value to others, too. Give everyone a chance to speak. Attend a mastermind group. Most are happy to allow prospective members to sit in on a meeting. Try as many groups as you can find that fit your needs. In the end, you might have to start your group. A mastermind group can significantly speed up your progress, help define your purpose, and give you a direction to make the most significant impact in your life and career.

20

THE POWER OF MENTORING & COACHING

The common area in leadership development is leveraging mentors to build capacity in the individual. It's commonly used in different capacities, depending on the existing need. In personal development, mentorship can tremendously impact someone's personal capabilities and increase our potential. When you need a bit of a boost to help you move forward, will you look for a mentor or a coach? It can be unclear what the differences between the two are, but there are some very important ones you need to know. From goals, relationships, expectations, and evaluations, there are major differences between coach vs. mentor.

Instead of viewing mentorship and coaching as different, you can look at them as two different styles with the same outcome. Whether you decide to utilize coaching or mentorship, it depends on your specific circumstances. With both mentoring and coaching, you can develop your skills, improve your performance, maximize your potential and become the person you want to be with the help of someone. There's a psychological process involved in mentorship, with guidance provided by someone much more experienced than you. The process helps to develop your purpose and align the craft personality.

Coaching and mentorship should take place on a daily and weekly basis. To have a lasting impact, it needs to have a more focused discussion geared towards something specific and agreed-upon goals from the beginning–ingredients of a quality and good mentorship process.

A LEARNING AGREEMENT

An agreement in which both of you clarify your objectives and expectations and the time frame needed throughout the mentoring relationship.

PURPOSEFUL CONVERSATIONS

You need to have meaningful, constructive, and structured conversations. That is when you get to know each other, work out the goals of your relationship, set parameters for your inter-actions and start to communicate and learn and connect with each other. When you do this, it will give your mentor the oppor-tunity to make changes and amend the benefits of achieving your goals and your purpose.

EMPOWERING

Good mentoring should consider the relational, emotional, and intellectual dimensions of the mentee. The coach should be solely focused on increasing your capacity and building your strength to enhance your development.

TRUST

Having trust between the mentor and the mentee is an absolute necessity for great impacts. Mentors need to foster a sense of safety in the relationship. There should be an atmosphere that breeds openness so you can engage easily and feel comfortable talking about private issues in an open and non-judgmental way.

FLEXIBILITY IN APPROACH

Depending on your situation, mentoring should be able to adapt and address the challenges that you face. So, if you are in a mentoring and coaching relationship, and the circumstances in which you first started have changed, your mentorship and guidance should reflect that. In times of crisis and uncertainty, it's often about dealing with what's in front of you and being flexible in achieving your goals.

Coaching and mentoring are essential ingredients to succeed in today's world. They create a meaningful and concrete shift in people and encourage the transfer of knowledge from the coach/mentor to the individual. Every day, we see the magic of mentoring. Whether it is in developing or engaging future and current leaders, the results are not in limited supply. The statistics say it all:

- 71% of Fortune 500 companies utilized mentoring programs as part of their growth strategy. Why? Because it pays off in performance, innovation, and productivity when you invest in leadership capability (Centre for Workplace Leadership 2016). *1000 employees were studied in five years (Gartner, 2006):*
- 25% of the employees had a salary-grade change because they participated in a mentoring program compared to only 5% of those who did not.

- Mentees have five times more promotions than those not in a mentoring program.

Coaching and mentoring benefits are mostly long-term and purpose-oriented. Mentoring will help you become more confident and enhance your self-esteem. It will motivate and inspire you to engage in your passions. In certain circumstances, mentoring will increase your self-awareness and make you more focused on the impact that you can make in the world through your work and your life.

Mentorship develops people, their thought process, and problem-solving skills, which is critical to completing your daily tasks. Coaching and mentoring can improve your work performance, help you find happiness, and change your attitude on everything that you do. Mentoring has had a profound impact on my personal life. I have used mentoring as a tool to develop and help me achieve my goals. Over the past 15 years, I have engaged in mentoring and coaching to overcome specific challenges or obstacles while fulfilling my life purpose.

So after my first two mentors that I mentioned earlier in the book, I started working with a coach during the 2008 and 2009 economic recession. My organization was struggling financially, and it was pretty challenging getting a hold over everything happening around me. We had to take a critical decision to either move the organization forward by laying off staff or close it down completely. I was about to get married at that time and start a new life, but I needed help balancing it. With the help of a mentor, I was able to have a grip over my mind and deal with what was in front of me, getting enough clarity to take action. I steered my organization in the right direction and increased our growth level. Again, I raised enough funds to stay afloat and thrive for years to come. The credit goes to my mentor, who provided the support that kept me going, and things were put in perspective. The incident set the stage for building a new life, alongside the experience of being present and married.

Many mentors have crossed my path, helping me build my business and mindset. I learned to become a coach myself. My most recent and more consistent mentor is Brian—a former executive who has consistently shown up in my life and business and has even come into coaching my team. Brian taught me how to silence my mind—as many thoughts jostled for supremacy. During my moments of silence, I've been able to learn how to be very present. When you're being present, you're ready to gain a lot of perspectives to focus on the task and not be too attached to the outcome. I never paid a dime to be mentored; they were based on quality relationships. My mentors are older and more experienced, and were keen to help me grow. They've achieved a certain level of success, and part of their success moving forward is giving back.

Some of my coaches are people that I've paid and have taught me something concrete. I used paid coaches to learn a skill, which dramatically accelerated the achievement of my goals. For instance, let's say you wanted to make $10,000 in a month as an entrepreneur; you can find someone who has been successful in your field that you can pay to teach you. If you wanted to learn how to become a professional photographer or start a photography business, you could find someone who has done it already and coaches aspiring professional photographers.

There are even informal ways of mentoring and coaching. Like for instance, if you can't afford to pay a coach, you can read books and follow people on social media who will openly mentor you for free every day. They even create a community around their mentoring. The first time I heard of this was from one of my early mentors, and he was a professional and motivator speaker. He introduced me to the work of Napoleon Hill— his book, *Think and Grow Rich*. That book changed my life. This mentor said he was a student of Napoleon Hill. And when I say "student," I mean he was someone who studied all of his work. Napoleon Hill has lots of books, videos, and tapes, and you can get informal mentoring through them. There are also lots of people who are alive today that have achieved a certain level of success. You can search using different hashtags or look at the New York Times bestseller list to see the larger influencers and thought leaders. Follow them on social media; you can connect to a community of people like them, learn from them, and discuss the content they put out daily.

PART III
TRANSITIONING TO YOUR LIFE PURPOSE

PREFACE

According to Dr Stephen R. Covey, "Your most important work is always ahead of you, never behind." It is self-explanatory and pretty much explains what we need to keep in mind to get to our desired destination. "Begin with the end in mind" means starting each day, task, or even project with a clear vision of your destination, then continue by doing the needful to make things happen. Everyone is mortal. There will be a time when you'll have to leave this world—when you'll die, regardless of whether you live your purpose or not. When you live with the end in mind, you fulfill and align your life with your purpose. You'll have to live in a way where, in the end, everyone will have something positive to say about your achievements, your character, and your contributions to this world. Having this in mind will help enhance your understanding of your purpose and how you fulfill it.

So, what exactly does it mean to live with the end in mind? It means you have a picture, a paradigm of the end, or an image and a point of reference in which you examine everything in your life. Keeping that in mind, you can be sure that whatever you do daily will not change your overall purpose. Like someone about to embark on a road trip with the destination in their head, so should your life. This means that you need to know where you want to go to better understand where you are now and what actions you need to head in the right direction. People succeed at something, and it doesn't mean anything to them. It's only then that they realize that success came at the expense of something that was way more important or valuable to them.

They make important sacrifices, but again, something that doesn't mean much. People from different walks of life, careers and industries want to achieve a certain level of recognition, income or professional achievement. What many don't realize is that their desire to reach these goals can blind them to the things that matter most. A lot of people don't see it until it is too late. True success will be very clear when you understand the legacy you want to leave behind at the end of your life.

If you don't have any self-awareness and don't become responsible for your thoughts, you're allowing people outside of your circle of influence to determine where your life goes—and it happens by default. If you want to awaken your true purpose, stop living by the playbook and scripts handed to you by your friends, family and other people's motives and agendas. These playbooks and scripts are people's ideology and are not based on principles and values that are personal to you and, therefore, cannot lead you to your purpose.

Since we've been bombarded with other people's ideas on how to live life, writing our life scripts is seen as a scripting process. By developing more self-awareness, we can discover some scripts that don't serve us but are deeply embedded in our lives. These scripts are not congruent with who we want to be. You and only you are responsible for writing them, and they are more rooted in values and principles that are near and dear to you.

The best way to develop your purpose road map is by writing your mission statement. Your mission statement should be focused on who you want to be, the impact you want to make, the values you live by and the character and achievements found in your life. To write a more meaningful personal mission statement, you have to start at the center of your circle of influence. It allows you to deal with your values and visions to help you mentally create the life that you were meant to live.

21

SETTING GOALS THAT FUEL YOUR PURPOSE

S etting goals lay the foundation for bringing your purpose to life and finding success. Goals help us focus our actions and energy on a result and enable us to measure the progress towards fulfilling our purpose. I think most people acknowledge that there is a gap between setting goals, developing plans, and communicating the goals to make a difference. There's lots of research that shows there is a link between performance goal setting and motivation. Along with imposing goals on yourself, leverage the setting of goals as a tool to create a sense of direction so that you reach your purpose. The goal-setting environment is crucial because it provides the conditions necessary to be effective with your action.

Goals and purpose are not synonymous. Goals are a finite accomplishment and serve your ultimate purpose. Some of your wider goals in life may be inspiring people to take better care of their environment. A goal could be as satisfying as organizing a cleanup campaign in the local park or as simple as teaching your kid to switch off the light when they leave the room; a goal will help you honor this purpose. The goals you set are a reflection of your purpose and give you the framework to measure your performance's quality, quantity, and rate. Setting goals always creates discrepancies because of the gap between where you are and where you want to be. Also, goal-setting affects our motivation, belief systems, and capabilities to perform. The gap between where we are and where we want to be should create the right motivation to be persistent, resilient, and help us leverage sustainable behaviors needed to reach our goals.

Three conditions need to be met if our goal-setting process is going to motivate us.

1. It would help if you had a commitment to your part in this process. This means that you need to do whatever it takes when it comes to achieving your goals. If you lack commitment, you lack motivation.
2. Your goals need to be specific and unambiguous. This will make it easier to assess your progress and adjust when needed.
3. It would be great if you had goal-directed behavior and happiness.

When it comes to your goals, making them action-oriented is the key to achieving them. If you don't have a goal-directed action, it'll be impossible for you to achieve your purpose. There are some useful tools that you can use to put goal-setting to work. They consider the human dynamic, and they help us generate goals that lead us to purposeful and effective behavior.

SELF-EFFICACY

The concept of self-efficacy is fundamental in setting and achieving goals. Efficacy is the belief that you hold about your ability to perform a specific task. These beliefs will affect how we set goals, as well as the choices that we make about the activities we engage in. Efficacy can also refer to the length of time one can persist in the face of challenges. Setting short-term and sub-goals will raise your self-efficacy instead of comparing it to an environment where only long-term goals exist. Your goals should be clear, challenging, and have a target and a time frame. Your self-confidence should be at the level of the difficulty of your goal.

TASK COMPLEXITY

You want to make sure that you include some short-term goals and that you have complex tasks, as they provide you with incentives and guidelines for a better outcome and performance. When your goals are long-term, they are too far from what needs to be achieved day-to-day and are difficult to connect with. Goal-setting requires realistic expectations, strategies for accomplishing the task, and subject-specific knowledge.

GOAL COMMITMENT

"If you make the unconditional commitment to reach your most important goals, if the strength of your decision is sufficient, you will find the way and the power to achieve your goals." Robert Conklin

When you commit to your goals, the relationship between your performance and the goals dramatically increases. When your goals are more complicated, your commitment levels need to be raised to sustain the effort required to meet them. The two main factors that you need to maintain and keep close to your heart are prioritization and self-belief. You have to believe that you'll reach the goals you've set and know what your priorities are. Ultimately, you need to link your goals to a bigger picture to achieve them.

FEEDBACK

Feedback is another crucial factor in setting your goals. Getting timely feedback will give you the right information and a sense of direction, ensuring that it aligns with your purpose. When you work with feedback, it indicates that you are paying attention to your progress in achieving the goals you've set for yourself.

SATISFACTION

You get more satisfaction in your life when you meet and surpass your goals. As you gain more success, your satisfaction grows. You need to create more challenging goals in your life to obtain satisfaction. There's no gain in saying that it improves your interest when you set more challenging goals and uncover the pleasurable parts of accomplishing the task associated with those goals.

Purposeful people are proactive. You are responsible for your life—no one else is and will be. You are an embodiment of all the decisions that you've made and not your conditions. You're the only person responsible for taking the initiative to turn your life around and make things happen for it. Proactive people are very well aware of their purpose, and they know that the conditions and circumstances are not to be blamed but rather the behavior that holds them back from reaching their full potential.

> *"So, each time a person decides to wait for 'time to change things', he or she is actually waiting for other people to change his or her fortunes."*
> — Innocent Mwatsikesimbe

You need to act and not wait to be acted upon. You need to take action and not have somebody taking action for you. If you keep waiting for someone to do the needful before you take action, you'll never achieve your purpose. Your conscious choices impact your behavior, and it's based on your values. We are naturally proactive beings, and our lives are conditioned by the circumstances that we've lived through. Because of this, we've made certain life decisions and consciously or unconsciously allow our circumstances to empower those that control us. Being reactive is the opposite of being proactive. A responsive person is affected by their physical environment more than their values and beliefs. A perfect example is when the weather is beautiful; it tends to impact our daily lives positively. Our attitude and performance aren't affected. However, when the weather is terrible, it affects their performance and attitude.

Proactive people take their destiny and purpose into their own hands. Rain or shine, it makes no difference for proactive people. Their values drive them, and they will continue to produce high quality and impactful work as fast as possible. You'll need to lower your impulses. True value is central to your existence if you want to live a more purposeful life. Even though external forces may influence you now and then, your response to those external forces should be value-based. To remain on this worthy path, you'll need to acknowledge that your choices are responsible for where you are today.

Another aspect of life is that it is naturally programmed to act and not be acted upon. Ultimately, we have the power to choose our responses to the events around us. Being an initiative-driven person has nothing to do with being pushy, obnoxious, and aggressive. Instead, it has everything to do with recognizing our ability to make things happen for ourselves. Many people wait around for something to happen and for someone else to take good care of our problems. Starting a business or a new career should be tied around your passion. That way, you'll be willing to stay committed while enjoying every bit of it for the long haul. Again, you'll want to take the initiative to find creative solutions to the problems that you want to solve.

There's a big difference between people who will take the initiative and those who will sit on the fence with their arms folded—they will never take action. If you want to find your purpose, you don't have to pay to find it. However, a lot of people don't take advantage of the opportunities in front of them. You can create a proactive environment in your life by being creative and resourceful. If you're reading this book, don't make excuses to be at the mercy of your situation.

One way to be more aware of your proactivity is to figure out where you spend most of your time. These days, there's so much happening in our daily lives. One way to separate things that we have no mental or emotional control over is by creating a circle of concern. By examining things in and out of your circle of concern, you'll get a clear perspective of what you have no control over. For the ones that you can control, put them into another smaller circle of influence. When you determine the time and energy spent between the circle of concern and your circle of influence, you can discover the degree of your proactivity. People who are more proactive in their lives care about their life purpose and focus their time and energy on those things in their circle of influence. They only concentrate on things they have control over.

Reactive people are more focused on the circle of concern. They focus on the problems regarding the environment, people, and circumstances beyond their control. They are more likely to be confused, overwhelmed, and with no purpose. The issue of self-blame and being resentful of other people will rear its head. They have accusing attitudes, make excuses, use reactive languages, and increased feelings of victimization.

When you're working inside the circle of concern and concentrate on the attributes, accomplishing anything will be very difficult. But if you shift focus to start concentrating on the circle of influence, you will generate positive energy that will influence your actions. You'll get inspired as you realize you can affect your situation based on your response to circumstances. There's a section of your chemical formula that you can change, and you can alter the nature of the results. If you want to find your purpose in life and improve your situation, concentrate on things that you have control over.

22

LEVERAGING POSITIVE
VISUALIZATION

W hen you practice daily positive visualizations, you can
take out blockages caused by our negative beliefs. Most
of these dark thoughts result from past trauma, which attacks
lives, causing pain and chaos. Anchored to past trauma, we
cannot push on. We typically come back to times in our lives
when intense feelings like pain and anxiety create a cognitive
stumbling block, which hinders our potential happiness. We can
set the stage for a more positive future journey by letting go of
the past and set the course for a safer and more fulfilling life.
Our mental creations aren't capable of seeing the difference
between the real and the imagined. So, if you come up with
something in your mind, which affects your body, your brain
cannot distinguish if it's real or a figment of your imagination.

Like any mental or physical process, visualization needs
foundation. You need to understand that the sensory qualities are
the strongest and that what your mind perceives is either visual
or auditory. If you bring a memory to the thoughts and feelings
of past successful events, you'll start to understand the various
patterns or traits that let you act in a particular way, which led to
similar circumstances and situations. This is proof that your

thoughts can create changes with the aid of visualization and imagery.

Creative visualization is a process that uses your imagination and your mind to make significant changes in your life and push you towards your purpose. When using creative visualization, you shape your habits, circumstances, character and subconsciously attract opportunities and people you most desire in your life. The images and thoughts that are most repeated will have the biggest effect on your mind and make those things happen. Your subconscious mind significantly impacts your actions, reactions, habits, and desires. They also attract similar results and circumstances. Your mind will create mental scenarios of specific incidents and events through creative visualization in your life.

The more you feed your thoughts with the right imagery, the stronger they become. Your imagination is one of the most important and influential ways to stimulate your creative visualization. Just think of the most amazing technologies that result from creative visualization, from cars to computers and even construction.

To live a more purposeful life, you'll need to bring and adapt visualization to your skillset. Just like learning how to ride a bike or learning an instrument, you need a lot of patience and persistence and also a support system. For the true benefits of visualization, you'll need discipline, time and practice to perfect the process. It's hard to say when you can start seeing the results for visualization. It also takes a lot of personal determination to push through it. Some experts say that you need 15 to 30 minutes a day of creative visualization. As you start to master the skill and get more comfortable with the idea of visualizing your result, you can reduce the amount to just a few minutes a day.

To get full effects, you need to be in a relaxed state for visualization to work. When your body is relaxed, your mind is so comfortable that you can get a sense of clarity and unconscious focus to be free—and that allows your mind to get to work. Various techniques can be used in combination with visualization and imagery to get your desired feeling and give you a sense of direction for purpose. One of the most common is called guided visualization. It involves visualizing your purpose that you want to achieve and then imagining yourself through the process of achieving it. When you combine your mental images with the emotions, it will start leading to the results that you need, and it can help you overcome any barriers to achieving your purpose. By simply repeating the same thoughts every single day, you can start to program your mind to bring visualization into the real world.

Creative visualization greatly helped me when I first started my organization, STOKED. My biggest challenge was raising money because I had never done anything like that before. I knew how to put together a program intuitively—the experience at the nonprofit where I worked came in handy. I understood how it worked. So as I embarked on the fundraising journey, I started getting more and more rejections and people ignoring my request, but I needed to visualize the result. The result for me was looking at a bus full of kids and mentors who were about to go snowboarding, where I was addressing them. I also imagined myself taking a chairlift, sitting next to kids and mentors while talking about life. It didn't end there; it included having fun and learning more about each other to grow and make a bigger impact on the world.

I also had a fundraising objective to raise $40,000—this is where it gets interesting. I created a vision board, where I put pictures of people snowboarding up on the wall; I also watched snowboard videos all the time in between work. I put pictures of coach tour buses, including chairlifts, because those are the things that I would need to get my organization off the ground. Any time I got a challenge or an obstacle in front of me, I would look at those images that I put together. I'd also lay in bed for at least 20 minutes before I got up, and I programmed my mind that today was going to be a great day while I visualized myself on a bus full of kids and mentors leaving the city, going to the mountains to snowboard. I kept replaying this over and over again in my mind. And then I even changed all my passwords to "raise40k." So, as I logged into my email and my various online accounts multiple times a day, I knew that I needed to raise $40,000 to get my program off the ground.

So, here's where the magic happened: I ended up raising $12,000 for the first snowboard program. I also ended up doing a skateboarding and surfing program, then finally, a skateboarding program in the fall. I realized that I raised a whopping $39,995 for the first-year programs, serving 45 kids throughout the year. Incredible, isn't it? The success was a hard-fought one—with hard work and my creative visualization technique playing a key role in getting my organization off the ground.

23

PERSONAL MANAGEMENT FOR PURPOSEFUL LIVING

Personal management is an integral part of the process of living your purpose. It helps direct and establish you on the right path towards your ultimate destination. A simple way to put it is that personal management is the planning, organizing, coordinating, and directing the various aspects of your life to hit your life's purpose. You need to have a strong and independent will to manage yourself.

> *"If you manage yourself, you control the flow of your time to the right direction. It takes self-discipline to be at the center of control for your own time."*
> -Israelmore Ayivor

Now imagine this - wake up every day at the same time. Don't let your life be dominated by the mattress. For some people, it is a ritual at 6:00 am. Manage your energy. Energy is one of the most powerful resources. Exercise and good diet. Be cheerful. Focus on the things you have, not what you don't have. Having a positive attitude is a choice. Read your WHY and your personal mission statement. Envision your purpose in your mind.

Hang on to it! Then a vision for what you'd like to look like at age 70. Practice a DO—REST—LEARN daily cycle, not just DO—REST. Learn something new as each day passes, and if possible, take note of it in your diary. Does the above information make sense? You can start managing your life this way and see what happens. It's all up to you. Personal management helps in building meaningful relationships with people while you pursue your passion and your purpose. You can break from your confines to live a more meaningful life with personal management.

There are five rules of self-management. You have failed to complete other assigned tasks after spending hours working on a complicated assignment. You pack up your bag and leave as soon as the clock hits five, without cleaning up all the mess. All the clutter you left on your desk, including the incomplete tasks, will come back to haunt you again the next morning when you sit at your desk. This is a perfect example of poor self-management.

There are four rules that you need to abide by to be an effective person who knows how to take control of their life and manage their personal and business affairs. These rules act as a personal guiding framework to work towards while you discover your purpose.

CREATE A MAP FOR YOUR LIFE

The first thing to do is to create a map for your life. It will allow you to understand yourself from a perspective of who you are, where you're coming from and where you're going. You will have an orientation of your direction and purpose. Mapping out your life is the core of every success you will attain in your life.

DOUBLE-CHECK YOUR ASSUMPTIONS

You need to review your assumptions. Everyone has some unique perspective or belief system that we use to assess ourselves. Some of these assumptions can hold you back from making progress, achieving your goals and finding lasting happiness. When you review them, you can look deep inside yourself, assessing your weaknesses and strengths.

SELF-ORGANIZATION

Organization is critical, and you need to apply it to yourself and your potential—if you want to achieve your desired goals. Without self-organization, even the skills that you have can be rendered useless and dissolved.

DEVELOPING YOUR SKILLS AND ABILITIES

You need to take your skills and abilities a notch higher. This includes introspection, self-awareness, willpower, and expanding your imagination. Disconnection will help you enhance your capacity to express yourself.

THE POWER OF A STRONG AND INDEPENDENT WILL

Your will is the ability to make choices and decisions and act in line with them. It's a very proactive way to deliver the program that you've crafted for your life. Your integrity measures the development and degree of your will for your life. The higher the level of your integrity, the stronger your will. Integrity is your ability to make commitments and follow through.

The best type of personal management requires you to prioritize your life. As a personal management expert, your discipline should come from within to organize the various aspects of your life. If you were disciplined to follow your value system, it would be of great benefit to you. When you're independent, it will give you the power to do something, even when you don't want to, as long as it aligns with your values. Develop your will by reaching and achieving small resolutions. This will give you the momentum and the excitement to create more substantial resolutions. You can boost your willpower by having a clear purpose, priorities, determination and proper planning.

TIME MANAGEMENT

Time management is an essential personal management skill. The scale of time management helps you organize and execute your task based on the time that you set for yourself. We each have 168 hours a week to accomplish tasks. How we use them determines the quality of our life and whether you succeed or fail. To effectively manage your time, you need to prioritize and discipline yourself. When a task is overwhelming, learning how to delegate responsibilities to capable and reliable people in your life will significantly give you more time. It will give you more time to focus on higher priority items and high-value tasks.

24

DEALING WITH NEGATIVITY

Negativity that bubbles up inside you or the world around can easily become toxic and prevent you from living the life you want. Have you ever struggled with negative thoughts? Of course, you have. If you have criticized yourself intensely or got caught up in stress, worry, depression or low self-worth, then you have had some of the symptoms. Even as you struggle with negativity, having a resilient mindset is critical. With that state of mind, you can draw strength from within and get back on your feet. Resilience is one of the most undervalued ways to find your purpose. When you can overcome difficulties and challenges while still maintaining the wellness of mind, a positive attitude and hope, you can fulfill your purpose.

People who are the most resilient keep their focus and emerge stronger after going through difficult situations. They also use their resilience as a model of success for others. As you move towards your purpose, you'll realize that you will face many challenges that will require you to have self-confidence and enhance your coping skills to help you pull through. Resilience enables you to overcome any negativity that tries to steer you off your path. Resilient individuals display a specific personality that influences the way they view problems and how they tackle them. Here are the three qualities of a resilient person.

- **Optimism** is the first quality of a resilient person. When you believe things will get better based on the reality of the current challenges, then you're optimistic.
- **Independence** is your ability to make decisions in your life and align your actions without having to rely on other people giving you directions or telling you what to do.
- **Control and responsibility** are the calmness and inner peace you have when you believe that you will be able to do something and change the adverse circumstances that happened in life.

When you learn how to overcome negativity, you know that you're training yourself to think positively, even when you're going through a difficult or stressful situation. You'll have the ability to change your negative thoughts into more positive ones and find humor when everything seems to be going wrong. Even though the past was terrible, you can see the opportunities within present situations. You also know that your future possibilities are not going to be jeopardized just because the past was negative. You can stay present and allow you to have a perspective to take advantage of the opportunities in front of you. Your purpose in life may not be a straight path, and you should be okay with that; we all know that life isn't about rainbows and unicorns and that it's the journey along the way and the lessons that you learn that will help you fulfill your life purpose. In bad times, our lessons are part of the process to fulfill our purpose.

It's important you develop a sense of resilience, and you have to take deliberate steps to enhance it and grow it. The first thing you need to do is formulate positive affirmations in your daily routine. Words are compelling. Whatever you speak can become a reality. If you talk positively about your life and what you want and who you are, you'll be amazed at how quickly it turns into a more favorable situation. Life will not always give you the easy way out. Strive for your purpose regardless of your current and surrounding circumstances. When you do, you'll increase your determination against all of the obstacles, and you will increase your resilience deposits too.

When you learn how to enhance your communication skills and build cultural bridges, you'll be able to express yourself and get the resources and help you need when faced with difficult circumstances. When it comes to facing some of these challenges, you'll need an accountability partner or community to lean on, and with better communication, you'll be able to get the mentorship that you need when you're facing a challenge in your life. Making decisions is an integral part of your daily life. As you're facing problems or obstacles, your ability to handle yourself with an open mind will help you get through those challenges, irrespective of how difficult they are. Doing this will help you maintain focus and maneuver towards your life purpose and goals.

Modern science helps us understand how the brain works biologically and how it impacts our ability to make it through difficult situations, as well as our determination and reasoning. Some parts of the brain produce chemicals that boost our happiness levels, while other parts bring out fear and anxiety. Be healthy, mentally, physically, and behaviorally. Even when situations are stressful, we need to reframe our perspective and thought patterns. Speaking to yourself on a subconscious level can unleash your potential to display resilience and stand firm, even when times are tough. Think positively about what you are doing to find a reason to continue forward as well as gain satisfaction and happiness.

25

LIVING A BALANCED LIFE

Most of us have a moment when we just feel out of whack with our lives. We feel like we've lost that sense of balance between work and life. We know we have been spending too many work hours a week, and the side effects are real. Then the crucial question becomes, what are we going to do about it? Measure against these four key dimensions for living a balanced life. The four dimensions: mental, physical, spiritual, and social will help you have a more healthy and balanced existence. You will improve your life and general outlook on your work in your purpose when you exercise all four on a daily basis. They will require time, proactivity and discipline to work.

THE PHYSICAL DIMENSION

The physical dimension is about taking care of your body, eating right, relaxing, exercising, and resting. Exercise is probably one of the most important. Although it's not urgent, most people understand the benefits of it but give it a very low priority. Time is always one of the biggest excuses for people not doing it. The best part is that you don't even need a lot of time; it's just 30 minutes a day, which isn't much. You can evolve by just having a daily practice, so go for a walk while you listen to a podcast that inspires you or listen to an audiobook that will get you on the path to finding your purpose. There are many benefits attached that it's almost silly not to take 30 minutes out of your day for a walk. I have a friend whose name is Libby Delana, and she's made a whole lifestyle around taking her "morning walk." She uses it as a time to meditate and self-reflect.

SPIRITUAL DIMENSION

At our core, we are spiritual beings, and we tend to incline to a higher power. If you picked up this book, then you believe that there's something bigger out there that is unseen or unheard that you know to exist. Whether you are religious or not, there's one spiritual practice that you can do, and that is meditation. Meditation is a basic practice within the spiritual dimension. Meditation helps to center, renew, strengthen, and reaffirm your commitment to be of service and fulfill your purpose in life. Nature has a way of showing its unique blessings to those who dive into its unique beauty. And meditation is one of the things that help us connect to a higher power.

THE MENTAL DIMENSION

Traditional education gives you mental development along with discipline. When you leave the rigorousness and structure of school, our minds tend to stop growing and atrophy. When we don't do personal and professional development or serious reading, we start to lose a sense of our passion for learning new things. We also stop thinking analytically or write as creatively as we used to when we were in school. It's important to come up with a continuous education curriculum for ourselves, based on our interests, passions, and, ultimately, our purpose.

To be a purposeful and proactive person, you have to find ways to continually educate yourself and train your mind as much as possible. You'll need to read good books that give you access to the most amazing minds of thought leaders, authors and philosophies to own and craft your mind to being the most ultimate purpose-driven individual. One way you could do that is by setting a goal to read a book proposed above. Book knowledge is one of the best types of knowledge that you can get aside from learning directly from the source. It's also important to remember that a person who doesn't read is no better off than a person who can't read.

THE SOCIAL DIMENSION

The social dimension is all about your interpersonal relationships, how you creatively collaborate and have empathetic communication with the people around you. Your social and emotional life is manifested through your relationships with other people, and they are often tied and woven together. Igniting your social dimension doesn't take much time because it can easily be done through communion with others. There's a pure joy in life when you are living your purpose, and you're aware of it. You want to make sure that you've lived your best life by the time you die.

26

THE NEXT STEPS

So, once you discover your purpose, it doesn't end there. When you finally know what gives your life meaning, you'll be very excited, pumped up, and passionate, but is that going to be enough to help you follow through with it? The next step in the process is to start to transition to your life purpose, and this is just the beginning. This means to start making changes, perhaps lots of changes and things that may be very uncomfortable. So how do you exactly transition?

SET AUDACIOUS GOALS

When you find your purpose, you know you have to set goals, as mentioned earlier. However, set audacious goals for that matter. If you have no audacious goals, your purpose won't mean much. It's just an ideology that isn't being put into action. You'll have to breathe life into this purpose. This is when you'll need to start planning how you are going to show your purpose to others.

As Carl Bard once said, "Though no one can go back and make a brand-new start, anyone can start from now and make a brand-new ending." This is where you start to make your ending come to life. For instance, one of the things I had to do to start transitioning to my life purpose when I started my organization was to end an engagement and sell a lot of my possessions at 28 years old and move back in with my family. In many ways, this felt like a really big step back, and I was often filled with a lot of regrets. A lot of people questioned my choices, including my family, and thought that I was going crazy for changing my life so drastically. I knew that I wanted to start this nonprofit organization and at least get my idea out into the world. For the first time in my life, I had so much clarity; I knew it would be tough, and I had no idea how tough it would be, but I was committed to the process.

So, when you find your purpose, you need to have that "project mentality." Your purpose should show up in something that comes to life out into the real world. Whether it's a website, book, movie, a new business, or in my cases, a cause, you have to set a deadline and put it out into the world. I started doing projects and announcing to the world that I would do it. It was my way of holding myself accountable and letting everybody know what I would do. I strive to be a person of integrity and go by my words. I would go ahead to implement all the changes above, and they were critical to my set goal. My nonprofit was paramount, and I put in all I had to make it come to life. To make it come to life, I set a deadline, rigorously pursued tasks and accomplished them—and, in the end, my nonprofit came to life!

You can't transition into your life purpose without having a vision, and if you don't have a vision, there's no way that you can succeed. Like the visualization part of this book, you have to begin with the end in mind, and you have to know that it's not going to be a straight path. Surround yourself with people that buy into your vision to facilitate it coming to life. Make sure it's so clear that no one could ever take you off your path. Without the goal and the vision, you're just going to be aimless and lose your motivation, drive, dream, and, ultimately, your purpose.

These are the exact steps you need to transition to your purpose. So, for me, money was one of the challenges to launching my nonprofit. I had put together a big list of people and came up with many different ways to make money, and I work on this every day. This will keep you motivated to transition to your purpose. It's perfectly fine if you don't achieve your goal because you don't know what your vision is. You'll learn to get better and more accurate and determined so that achieving your purpose gets easier over time. So once you figure out your purpose, the first thing to do is to keep in mind what will rear its ugly as you tend to progress.

A lot of people fail in their transition to fulfill their life purpose because of fear. There is so much fear around disappointing yourself, fear of those around you, fear of not being good enough, fear of failing, and fear of losing everything. There are so many questions that it's almost like they're swords hanging over your head. You're going to ask yourself; will I lose everything that I created or have up until this point? Will I be able to make a living on this new life purpose? Am I that good? Will I disappoint my family, my friends, and myself if I pursue my purpose? Does it all matter?

You shouldn't let others disliking, judgment, or fear of rejection stop you from fulfilling your purpose. Exactly how true is all of that? Aren't all of these questions going to stop you from being who you truly are? When you make that decision to transition to your life purpose, you'll find it easy. There will be so many times when you start to regret the decisions that you made. You want to go back to the life that you had before, only to realize that life was miserable, meaningless, or "safe."

There's a reason why you picked up this book, and there's a reason why you wanted to do something bigger in your life, and it's important to you. If things were going to be easy, everyone would be doing it and fulfilling their life purpose. It's not, and that's why a lot of people stay in the safe zone and wait until something drastic happens in the world to figure out that they have to make a change. Whether it is a recession, a pandemic, or a lot of uncertainty, a lot of people have questions right now, and there's no better time to make change than when there's a change in the world. The fear of leaving your old life behind pushes you away from your purpose. So many people have what they should be doing right in front of them, but they get so scared, and when they're much older, they live a life of regret. Life is too short to live a life based on other people's rules and paradigms. If the world feels uncertain, then the events of the day are constructed by people who sought them in their mind. If that's the case, then you have not chosen the world that you wanted. Reframe it and come up with your vision and do the work to find and fulfill your purpose.

Remind yourself why you took the first step, and you got started. It's going to keep you going. It will be so hard to steer clear of the people, including your family and friends, who will take you away from your purpose. It's going to take a lot of work to ignore them and stay away from negativity so that you can stay on this path. It also helps to find people and a community working towards the same vision, so you can keep yourself accountable. Take comfort in knowing that before I started this life path, even I didn't have the same friends that I had before I started. I have friends all over the world and in the United States who are pleased with my contributions to the world. I've traveled the world because of my purpose. Because of the things that I've done, I've gotten opportunities to share my message across the stages and other media outlets worldwide, all because I decided to do it. You may not necessarily need to sell your possessions or break an engagement to find and act on your purpose. However, some level of sacrifice is needed to let go of the things holding you back and the things that don't serve you well. At least for me, there was a moment of clarity that I never had in my life. It was a decision that I needed to make to advance forward.

Start making a list of all of the things holding you back and all the things that don't serve you. Whether it is expenses, your lifestyle, relationships or where you live, some of those sacrifices will be needed to get what you need to fulfill your purpose. Ultimately, realize that nothing will hold you back from achieving your purpose. Your current reality is formed by staying in your comfort zone. When giving up the things that hold you back and getting out of your comfort zone, things begin to align to meet your purpose.

HOW TO MAKE THIS TRANSITION

Finding your purpose seems a lot easier than actually working on it, correct? When you're searching for life purpose, you're just looking into yourself and finding what you need to do in life. The transition requires a lot of action. It is you doing something more than just thinking about it. How you're going to pay for it is important. Most people don't pursue what they truly want because they don't think that they can afford to live a life if they go for that dream job or business. The reality is, you need to build some level of financial security for your purpose. There were moments where I struggled financially, and if I were to do it all over, I would have focused on building more of the financial cushions to allow me to get to my purpose faster.

So, when I first started, I had enough money for three months. Knowing that I would be living with my family, I didn't have to pay rent, which helped a lot. It was only for three months, and it was a welcome change in my life. If I had the opportunity to do it over again, I would be cutting expenses as much as possible and looking for ways to save a lot of money to give me leverage to start pursuing my purpose. So, if I were to start over, my transition would be to get a side hustle, leveraging my skills while reading, learning, digesting and doing the work needed to find purpose. Keep in mind that the journey will take a while. It took 10 or 11 months from the time I came up with the idea to start my non profit. Once I made the decision, things moved much faster. For those that didn't put in the work, it took them twice or three times as long to reach their goals.

Finding your purpose is truly a life path, and I've been on this path for 15 years, so it's important to know that you need to be patient with yourself. If you have a job, stay at it and squirrel away as much money as possible. Then find a way to create additional income—there are so many ways you can achieve that and grow your skills. I'm a big proponent of your purpose somehow being entrepreneurial, so the best way to do it is first, learn your skills and then apply them to some side hustle. For me, even during that first year, it took another year before I was able to make a full-time salary & live off my nonprofit—so it took two years. Again, I would not change my path, knowing what I know now. Focus on building more financial security to give you more peace of mind in pursuing your purpose.

To transition to your life purpose, you need to have systems in place. When I was starting my nonprofit, I needed to have a nonprofit partner, a website, my fundraising platform, and all of those things. It's easy to get ideas off the ground, whether it is social media, online networking, online groups, and even various gig-economy-type websites like Fiverr or Upwork, where you can get things done very easily and cheaply.

It's important to remember that you don't have to do everything. You can find many people to help you. I just put out different ads online looking for volunteers or interns, and I had a lot of people that shared my vision and wanted to help out. I would start small and build out different projects and tasks, and you could either outsource them cheaply or ask people to volunteer. You'll be surprised how many people are looking for ways to contribute to projects. Other people are also searching for purpose, and they're searching for something they can use, such as your platform, to find it. I'd also build a community of like-minds. I'm big into building a community and using it as accountability for me to achieve my goals. When you enlist people into your accountability community, you help them grow as well. They act as a support system, and when you lean on them and tell them, "Hey, I need your help to fulfill my purpose," it gives them purpose as well.

Reframe your mind as to what kind of relationships you can have. You can have perfectly great relationships with people you have never met face-to-face. I connect with a lot of people online and build relationships from there. I know about their family and their friends, their ideas or beliefs and their values, and share the same vision. We're yet to meet in person, so we talk about what relationships would look like as it relates to fulfilling purpose. Once your purpose becomes clear, share it with the world and tell everyone about it. Build your brand around this idea. Read everything about it and share it with everyone you know to become an expert at it. Like musicians, artists, painters, authors don't hide away their purpose, they bring it out into the world.

Your purpose is a creative expression of yourself and your gifts. The best way you can display your purpose is by putting it out for the world to see. Slowly but surely, it will get there; the transition process will be a positive journey and will never have a final result. Give it your full time and attention, and watch it flourish and grow. You will become a better person, and the world will ultimately become a better place for all who fulfill their purpose.

AFTERWORD

Finding meaning and living your purpose is one of the most amazing and enjoyable experiences that you can have in life. Imagine waking up with the feeling that you want to make a big impact in the world, with your name reverberating across continents, all because of your contributions towards humanity. Wouldn't that feel great? When I think about the decision to pursue my purpose, I feel excited having gone this route regardless of the challenges. On the path to fulfilling purpose, I met my wife, and we now have three kids.

I started everything from scratch, and I have traveled the world to tell people about my purpose. I created opportunities for others and know that people have gotten married because of my life purpose. To think that my friend, Jyoti Folch-Berman, has a tattoo of my organization's logo makes me excited and proud. Even the 10,000 people that have been impacted by my work are the real MVPs—they mean so much to me, and I'm greatly honored to have served them. Words fail me to express my gratitude.

To know that my life is better and thousands of lives too because of what I was doing makes it all worth it. You never know who you'll impact and inspire by fulfilling your purpose. There's a ripple effect that happens. If I were told that I would have created a lifestyle to impact young people and that the idea would spread around the world, I would never have believed it. I think that's the point of having a purpose—it is to impact the world and those who need what you have to offer.

When you find that thing that gives you peace, you can start fulfilling it in you for as long as I have. There's a certain confidence that you have, knowing that even though things are very tough, you will persevere because you have built up the skills, relationships and the experience to draw upon. Then you'll find yourself in places that you never knew existed and be around people you used to think meeting was a mirage. There will be ups and downs, there will be struggles, and there will be times where you get depressed and have anxiety, but, ultimately, think about where you'd like to be compared to where you were before you started this journey. That is one thing that should keep you going.

You'll become a much stronger person. You'll have convictions; you'll be able to learn faster and connect with people with more developed and amazing interpersonal skills. In your quest to find your true calling, you'll need to focus on finding the things that motivate you. It's going to make you stop wasting time and doing things that won't sync with you and your full potential. It's disastrous to spend your time chasing after the wrong goals, whether in your business career or personal life; you'll need to find some quality time and ask yourself many soul-searching questions in the beginning. Reflect on life as much as possible, and start to re-engineer and recalibrate things when needed. If you want to get healthy in your purpose-filled life, eliminate the things that prevent you from being healthy. If you have great interpersonal skills and many relationships were broken in the past, start fixing.

One of the things you'll learn on this path is to take the time to evaluate the choices in front of you. It's also important to find what you're passionate about to focus your time and energy on the things that truly matter—it will keep you motivated and away from disappointment in your life. Remember that when you are in tune and in sync with the light that guides you, internally and externally, it will make the path so much clearer as you pursue your purpose. Explore and reach out for that "one thing" that makes all the difference—and you'll know when you find it. This is the life that you want to live; this is the impact you want to make. Follow the steps outlined in the book, so you can have a purposeful life and leave a legacy for the next generation.

Thank you so much for reading this book. Please go to lifepurposesecrets.com and join the community and conversation there.

ABOUT THE AUTHOR

Steve Larosiliere, is an award-winning entrepreneur and purpose coach who's passionate about helping others find their purpose. Since 2005, he has mentored and motivated young people and adults to increase their skills, relationships, and experiences to transform their lives and communities.

Steve has also worked with C-level executives, entrepreneurs, brands, and small businesses as a consultant and coach to increase their sales and impact their community. Steve started STOKED—a youth mentoring organization that has nationally impacted the lives of over 10,000 youth and mentors. Lastly, he speaks globally on subjects around how to find purpose, community engagement, and social entrepreneurship. Steve has a BA degree in History from Stony Brook University and earned his Master's in Public Administration from the School of Public Affairs at Baruch College. Steve lives in Chicago with his wife and three children.

You can join the community at:

LifePurposeSecrets.com

If you would like to learn more from Steve Larosiliere, please visit:

SteveLarosiliere.com